I0401379

Dear Reader,

I am pleased to present my book

Hacking Wifi:
A Starter's Manual

Hacking is a complex and fascinating field that may seem confusing to beginners.

In reality, it is a practice aimed at exploiting or diverting the use of a service/protocol/software or at finding vulnerabilities in computer systems. It can also encompass the development of tools/programs/exploits, ranging from bug bounty programs to the creation of devices such as signal jammers, data capture boxes, malicious USB keys, or other customized devices designed to exploit system vulnerabilities or security flaws.

First, we will review the fundamentals of hacking and computer security, so you can have a solid understanding of the key concepts before moving further. Once we have established these basics, we can explore various hacking techniques commonly used today.

In the first chapter, we will focus on the most classic WiFi attack, the dictionary attack against WPA/WPA2 protocols. We will also see how to protect against this attack.

In the second chapter, we will delve deeper by exploring a more sophisticated attack on a WiFi access point, the Rogue AP attack. We will review the techniques necessary to carry out this attack, as well as the preventive measures you can take to protect your network against such attacks.

In the following chapters, we will explore various local network attacks, such as MITB (Man-In-The-Browser), spoofing, and many others.

Finally, we will discuss the detection and exploitation of vulnerabilities.

I am convinced that this book will be an asset for those looking to learn more about hacking and cybersecurity, and I am excited to accompany you on this fascinating adventure.

Happy reading!

Julien B.

Disclaimer

I would like to emphasize that my book is in no way intended to encourage or promote computer hacking or any other illegal activities.

The information and techniques presented in this book are intended for educational or research purposes only and must be used responsibly and legally.

Any misuse or illegal use of the knowledge acquired from this book is strictly prohibited and may result in legal action.

It is the reader's responsibility to comply with all applicable laws and regulations regarding the use of the technologies presented in this book.

International Law Context

Computer hacking is considered a criminal offense in many countries and is governed by various international laws and agreements, including but not limited to:

The Council of Europe's Convention on Cybercrime (Budapest Convention): This treaty criminalizes a range of cyber activities, including unauthorized access, data interference, system interference, and misuse of devices. Signatory countries are required to implement these offenses in their domestic laws and provide international cooperation.

The European Union's General Data Protection Regulation (GDPR): While primarily focused on data protection and privacy, the GDPR includes provisions that can result in severe penalties for data breaches caused by hacking, impacting organizations operating within or dealing with EU citizens.

The United States Computer Fraud and Abuse Act (CFAA): This law penalizes unauthorized access to computer systems and has extraterritorial reach, meaning it can apply to actions outside the United States if they affect U.S. systems.

The United Nations Convention against Transnational Organized Crime (UNTOC): This convention addresses the international cooperation required to combat various forms of transnational organized crime, including cybercrime.

Penalties for computer hacking can include significant fines and lengthy prison sentences. Victims of cybercrime may also seek damages and compensation through civil litigation. It is essential to adhere to international and national laws and to use technology ethically and legally.

Glossary of Terms Commonly Used in Networking:

Router: A device that connects different computer networks and directs traffic between them.

Gateway: A device that connects different networks with different protocols.

Switch: A device that connects multiple network devices and allows them to communicate with each other.

Protocol: A set of rules and conventions governing how network devices communicate.

IP Address: A unique numerical address that identifies each device on a network.

DHCP: A network protocol that allows devices to automatically receive an IP address.

DNS: A system that translates domain names into IP addresses.

Firewall: A security device that filters incoming and outgoing network traffic.

VLAN: A Virtual Local Area Network that separates traffic based on function or group membership.

MTU: Maximum Transmission Unit, representing the largest data packet size a network can transmit.

NAT: Network Address Translation, which translates IP addresses between different networks.

OSI: Open Systems Interconnection, a reference model for communications between open systems.

SSL: Secure Sockets Layer, a security protocol for internet communications.

VPN: Virtual Private Network, which securely connects remote networks over the internet.

LAN: Local Area Network, a computer network that spans a limited geographical area.

DMZ (Demilitarized Zone): A security buffer zone between the internal network and external network, where devices are accessible from outside but with restrictions.

The Data Link Layer, also known as Layer 2 in the OSI model:

The Data Link Layer is a layer of the OSI model that sits between the Physical Layer and the Network Layer. This layer is responsible for the reliable transmission of data between two physically connected nodes, using error detection and correction techniques, as well as flow control and access control mechanisms for shared media. It also handles the encapsulation and decapsulation of data packets by adding and removing specific headers relevant to each protocol at this layer. The most commonly used protocols at this layer include Ethernet, Wi-Fi, and PPP (Point-to-Point Protocol).

The OSI Model, or Open Systems Interconnection:

The OSI model is a reference model that describes the necessary steps for data communication between computer systems, regardless of their architecture and internal functioning. This model consists of seven layers, each with a specific role in data transmission, starting from the Physical Layer which manages the electrical or optical signals sent over the transmission medium, up to the Application Layer which deals with data presented to the end user. The different layers of the OSI model are designed to be independent of each other, enabling interoperability between equipment from different manufacturers and using different technologies. This model is widely used to understand network communications and the security of computer networks.

Wi-Fi Glossary:

Wi-Fi: A set of wireless communication protocols based on the IEEE 802.11 standard, enabling high-speed data transmission between devices.

Access Point (AP): A network device that creates a Wi-Fi network by emitting radio signals for Wi-Fi clients to connect to.

SSID: Service Set Identifier, the name given to a wireless network.

BSSID: Basic Service Set Identifier, the MAC address of the Access Point (AP) which broadcasts the wireless signal.

AP: Access Point, the wireless access point that allows devices to connect to the network.

Channel: The frequency used by a Wi-Fi network to transmit wireless data. Available channels vary by country and radio spectrum regulator.

Spoofing: A technique in computer security used to impersonate another person or device by falsifying information such as IP address or MAC address.

Rogue AP / AP spoofing: A fraudulent access point configured to mimic a legitimate access point to lure users into connecting to it.

Packet Injection: A technique allowing an attacker to send malicious data packets to a wireless network to compromise its security.

Dictionary Attack: A method used by hackers to guess passwords using a list of commonly used passwords or by creating a customized list.

Handshake: A security procedure where an access point and a wireless client exchange information to establish a secure connection.

WEP: Wired Equivalent Privacy, an outdated security protocol used to protect wireless networks. It is considered insecure and easily exploitable by attackers.

WPA: Wi-Fi Protected Access, a newer security protocol used to protect wireless networks. It offers better security than WEP and uses stronger encryption algorithms.

Encryption: A process of transforming data into an unreadable format to protect data confidentiality.

Sniffing: A technique used by hackers to intercept data flowing over a wireless network without being detected.

Hacking Glossary:

Denial of Service Attack (DDoS): An attack aimed at making a website or service unavailable by flooding the server with requests.

Botnet: A network of compromised devices (e.g., computers infected with malware) that can be remotely controlled to carry out attacks.

Exploit: A technique or program that takes advantage of a vulnerability or security flaw in a system.

Firewall: A software or hardware device that filters network traffic to protect a network from attacks.

Ethical Hacking: The practice of testing computer systems for vulnerabilities, often for security purposes and with the owner's permission.

Social Engineering: The art of deceiving or persuading people to obtain confidential information or access to systems.

Malware: Malicious software designed to damage or gain unauthorized access to computer systems.

Phishing: A technique that deceives users into believing they are interacting with a trusted entity to obtain personal information such as login credentials or credit card numbers.

SSL/TLS: Encryption protocols that secure communications over the Internet by establishing encrypted connections between servers and clients.

Spoofing: A technique that masks the identity or location of a computer to deceive a system or user.

Zero-day: A security vulnerability not yet known to software vendors and for which no patch is available.

MITM (Man-in-the-Middle): An attack that intercepts and modifies communications between two parties to eavesdrop or manipulate exchanged data.

IP Spoofing: A technique that allows an attacker to hide their real IP address by falsifying the source address of an IP packet.

Firewall Bypass: A technique to circumvent firewall security rules by exploiting system vulnerabilities or using bypass techniques such as tunneling.

Ah, the foundations of hacking! This is where it all begins, isn't it?

You must understand wireless communication protocols and technologies to succeed in hacking.

This means having a deep understanding of different types of networks, their functionalities, security protocols, and vulnerabilities.

Without a solid grasp of these foundations, succeeding in the field of hacking can be challenging. And believe me, the most talented hackers all started by learning the fundamentals before moving on to more advanced attacks. So, are you ready to dive into this exciting world and learn more about hacking?

Even for cybersecurity experts, it's always good to review the basics from time to time to keep skills and knowledge up to date. Technologies evolve rapidly, new security protocols are introduced, vulnerabilities are discovered, and attackers are becoming more sophisticated.

Therefore, understanding the basics of hacking is crucial to keeping up with current trends and being able to defend against the latest attacks. In the chapter on fundamentals, you will discover the essential principles of networks, different types of wireless networks, common security protocols, and the most frequent vulnerabilities. This will help you build a solid foundation to progress in the field of wireless hacking.

So, are you ready to begin?

If you are passionate about cybersecurity and hacking, then you are in the right place!

In this book, I will guide you through the fascinating world of hacking and cybersecurity, providing you with the essential foundations to start progressing in this field.

However, theory alone is not enough. To truly understand the concepts we will cover, I strongly recommend setting up your own testing lab. Rest assured, this does not require a significant time investment or cost.

You can easily create a small testing lab with a laptop running your preferred Linux distribution, two virtual machines, or even an old PC repurposed for the occasion. You can also use your phone to test certain attacks.

The advantage of setting up a testing lab is that you can have fun creating attack and defense scenarios.

You can also participate in challenges and "Capture The Flag" (CTF) competitions, where participants must find security vulnerabilities in computer systems and exploit them to retrieve information or flags.

By creating your own testing lab, you will gain practical experience and have a better understanding of the concepts we will cover in this book. You will also develop your hacking and cybersecurity skills.

On the next page, you will find ideas for scenarios.

I strongly encourage you to set up your own testing lab and participate in challenges and CTFs.

This will allow you to put into practice the concepts you will learn in this book and gain practical experience in hacking and cybersecurity.

Happy reading and happy hacking!

Chapter 1:

The Basics

Chapter 1: Basics

The Basics of Wi-Fi Networks

Wireless networks are becoming increasingly common today, offering greater flexibility and mobility compared to traditional wired networks. However, their security can be vulnerable to attacks, leading to severe consequences such as the leakage of sensitive data or identity theft.

In this book, we will focus on the WPA and WPA2 security protocols for Wi-Fi networks, as they are still widely used today. The WEP security protocol is obsolete and considered ineffective in terms of security because it is very easy to compromise.

In this chapter, we will also explain the basics of Wi-Fi network communication, including ARP and DHCP protocols, as well as the structure of a Wi-Fi packet.

We will also examine the different types of authentication used by Wi-Fi networks, such as WPA/WPA2, and the vulnerabilities associated with them.

Understanding these basic concepts is essential to setting up effective attacks and better protecting against Wi-Fi hacking attacks.
In this book, we will focus on two particularly effective types of Wi-Fi attacks on WPA/WPA2 encryption.

The first attack: dictionary attack uses a list of passwords to try to guess the network password. Hackers often resort to this method because it is quick and easy to implement. To carry out this attack, we will mainly use the aircrack-ng suite and cupp3, a custom password generator.

To successfully perform a dictionary attack, it is essential that the password is weak.

The second attack is the rogue AP attack, also known as the malicious access point attack. This attack involves creating a fake access point that mimics a legitimate access point to trick users into connecting to the malicious network. This technique is often used to steal sensitive information such as login credentials, credit card data, etc. We will also use aircrack-ng to capture the handshake of the target network and try to exploit it with our rogue AP.

Chapter 1: Basics

Wireless networks operate using radio waves to transmit data between connected devices. These radio waves are emitted by access points (APs) or wireless routers and are captured by the wireless adapters

Wireless networks are identified by their service set identifier (SSID), which is a unique identifier assigned to each wireless network. SSIDs can be hidden for security reasons, but this does not make them invisible to attackers.

They use communication protocols such as the Transmission Control Protocol (TCP) to ensure data transmission. These communication protocols can be subject to vulnerabilities that can be exploited by attackers.

The handshake is an important part of the communication between a device and a wireless access point.

In networks using WPA or WPA2 encryption, it is possible to capture the handshake to attempt to exploit it and compromise the network's security. Attackers can use specific tools to capture the handshake, then use it to try to guess the network password using dictionary attacks or other methods. The handshake is a process that occurs when a device connects to a password-protected wireless network. During the handshake, the device and the access point (AP) negotiate an encryption key that will be used to encrypt the data exchanged over the network.

Can also fall victim to rogue AP attacks. Attackers can create a fake AP or a malicious access point to intercept data sent by users. By understanding how wireless networks work and the vulnerabilities that can affect them, it is possible to take measures to protect networks and data.

Chapter 1: The Basics

The Importance of Wireless Network Security and Best Practices

Wireless network security is crucial for protecting sensitive data. However, these networks have many vulnerabilities, making attacks common and dangerous. Understanding these risks is key to improving protection. Attackers can intercept wireless transmissions and access unprotected data. Security flaws in protocols like WEP or WPA also enable attackers to compromise network security.
Here is a list of the most significant risks associated with WiFi hacking:

- **Intercepting Wireless Transmissions:** Attackers can easily intercept wireless transmissions and access private data if it is not protected. This can include information such as passwords, credit card numbers, emails, files, and more.

- **Accessing Unsecured Wireless Networks:** Unsecured wireless networks are easy to access and can be a goldmine for attackers. They can easily access data stored on computers and devices connected to the wireless network.

- **Security Flaws in Encryption Protocols:** Encryption protocols such as WEP or WPA may have security flaws that attackers can exploit to compromise network security.

- **Denial of Service (DoS) Attacks:** DoS attacks can render a wireless network unusable by sending a massive amount of traffic to the network, saturating it, and preventing legitimate users from connecting.

- **Phishing Attacks:** Phishing attacks are a common method used by attackers to trick users into thinking they are connecting to a legitimate wireless network when, in reality, they are connecting to a network controlled by the attacker.

- **Packet Injection Attacks:** Packet injection attacks are a common method used by attackers to send malicious packets into a wireless network. This can include the injection of viruses, malware, and other types of malicious programs.

- **Dictionary Attacks:** Dictionary attacks are a method used by attackers to guess passwords using lists of commonly used words and their variations. Weak and common passwords can easily be guessed by attackers using this technique. Therefore, it is important to choose strong and complex passwords that are harder to guess.

- **Rogue AP Attacks:** Rogue AP attacks involve creating a malicious access point that mimics a legitimate access point. Users who connect to this malicious access point can fall victim to phishing attacks or data theft.

Understanding these risks is essential to implement adequate security measures and protect against potential attacks. Best practices for wireless network security include using robust encryption protocols (such as WPA3), configuring strong and unique passwords, regularly updating software and firmware, and actively monitoring networks to detect any suspicious activity. By staying vigilant and adopting these measures, you can effectively protect your wireless networks against common and emerging threats.

However, best practices and good cyber hygiene can help strengthen wireless network security. Regular software updates, correct security settings configuration, and creating strong passwords are crucial measures to prevent attacks.

Here are some best practices:

- Use strong and unique passwords* for the wireless network and connected devices.

- Implement MAC filtering to allow only approved devices to connect to the network.

- Limit the number of available IP addresses in the DHCP lease to prevent saturation attacks.

- Use WPA2-PSK security configuration with AES encryption.

- Disable SSID broadcasting to make the network invisible to unauthorized users.

- Set up a separate guest Wi-Fi network with appropriate security rules and limited access.

- Regularly update the router firmware to fix security vulnerabilities.

- Monitor network traffic to detect any suspicious or unauthorized activity.

- Educate users about wireless network security and inform them of best practices.

Users must be aware of the risks and best practices to ensure network security. Human errors can often cause vulnerabilities in wireless networks, so it is essential to raise user awareness about these risks.

Strong passwords:
Strong passwords are complex and difficult to guess. They typically consist of a combination of upper and lower case letters, numbers, and special characters. Strong passwords are vital for wireless network security because they are harder for attackers to crack. It is recommended to use passphrases instead of simple passwords and to change them regularly.

Chapter 1: The Basics
How Wi-Fi Networks Work

When a device connects to a Wi-Fi network, it must first authenticate with the wireless access point (WAP) or AP by providing the appropriate credentials. The WAP then uses a communication protocol like DHCP (Dynamic Host Configuration Protocol) to assign an IP address to the device. Once an IP address is assigned, the device can communicate with other devices on the network.

Data sent over a Wi-Fi network is encapsulated in frames transmitted using the Data Link Layer protocol of the OSI model. Wi-Fi also uses the ARP (Address Resolution Protocol) to resolve the MAC addresses of devices connected to the network.

Wi-Fi operates on different radio frequencies, primarily 2.4 GHz and 5 GHz. The 2.4 GHz frequencies have a longer range but are more prone to interference, while the 5 GHz frequencies offer higher bandwidth but with a shorter range.

The security of Wi-Fi networks is crucial to prevent unauthorized access and data loss. Wi-Fi networks are often secured using encryption protocols such as WPA2 and by limiting access to authorized devices.

In summary, Wi-Fi is a widely used wireless communication protocol that provides wireless Internet connectivity to devices such as laptops, smartphones, tablets, and IoT devices. Wi-Fi networks work by using radio waves to transmit data between devices and using protocols like DHCP and ARP to manage connections and IP addresses.

The security of Wi-Fi networks is essential to prevent unauthorized access and data loss.

Understanding how Wi-Fi networks work and implementing appropriate security measures can effectively protect wireless networks.

The Address Resolution Protocol (ARP):

The Address Resolution Protocol (ARP) is used in networks to associate an IP address with a MAC (Media Access Control) address. IP addresses identify machines within the network, while MAC addresses identify the individual network interfaces of each machine.

When a device wants to communicate with another machine on the network, it needs to know its MAC address. To achieve this, it broadcasts an ARP request to all machines connected to the network, asking if any machine knows the MAC address of the target machine associated with the given IP address. If the target machine is present on the network, it responds with its MAC address, which is then stored in the ARP table of the requesting device. This ARP table prevents the need for sending ARP requests every time the device wishes to communicate with another machine.

ARP can also be maliciously exploited through ARP spoofing, where attackers send false ARP responses to deceive network machines and intercept traffic. Therefore, understanding how ARP functions and implementing appropriate security measures is crucial to protect the network from such attacks.

The Dynamic Host Configuration Protocol (DHCP):

The Dynamic Host Configuration Protocol (DHCP) is a network protocol used to automatically assign IP addresses and other network configuration settings to computers and other devices.

DHCP simplifies network administration by dynamically assigning IP addresses to devices, rather than requiring manual configuration which can be tedious and prone to errors. DHCP also centrally manages IP addresses in the network, reserving specific IP addresses for certain devices.

DHCP operates in a client-server model, where a DHCP server is configured to distribute IP addresses and other network configuration settings to DHCP clients. When a DHCP client connects to a network, it sends a request for an IP address allocation to the DHCP server, which responds with an available IP address from the configured IP address pool on the server.

Additionally, DHCP configures other network settings such as subnet mask, default gateway, and DNS servers. These settings are also distributed by the DHCP server to DHCP clients during the IP address allocation request.

DHCP is widely used in local area networks (LANs) to streamline the management of IP addresses and other network settings.

A WiFi packet
is the smallest unit of data transferred over a wireless network. It contains several fields used to route data between devices. Here's an explanation of the typical structure of a WiFi packet:

Header: The header is the first part of the packet and contains control information for data transmission, such as source and destination MAC addresses, sequence numbers, and error control codes. The header is divided into three subsections: control, duration, and address.

Packet Body: The packet body contains the actual data to be transferred. This can be any type of data, such as email packets, files, chat messages, etc.

FCS: The Frame Check Sequence (FCS) is a data integrity check value. It allows the receiver to verify that the data was correctly transmitted without errors.

The structure of a WiFi packet varies depending on the packet type. For example, data packets differ from management packets like scan packets or probe packets.

Understanding the structure of WiFi packets is important because it helps understand how data is transmitted over a wireless network and how attacks can be launched to compromise network security.

WiFi security largely depends on the encryption type used. WEP is considered obsolete and easily crackable. WPA and WPA2 are still widely deployed.

However, even WPA2 can be vulnerable to certain attacks, such as dictionary attacks. To enhance WiFi security, the WPA3 protocol has been developed and is considered more secure than previous versions.

It's important to note that many routers and access points do not yet support WPA3, so WPA and WPA2 remain the most common choices.

Therefore, it is crucial to take measures to secure your WiFi network, such as using strong passwords, regularly changing your security keys, disabling unnecessary features like WPS, and regularly monitoring your network activities to detect any suspicious activity.

Chapter 1:
The Basics

WiFi Network Encryption

WPA and WPA2 are two security protocols for wireless networks developed to replace the more vulnerable WEP protocol.

WPA (Wi-Fi Protected Access) was released in 2003 to enhance WiFi network security using the TKIP (Temporal Key Integrity Protocol) encryption protocol. TKIP was designed to address WEP weaknesses by employing dynamic key encryption that changes regularly and adding an integrity check mechanism to detect any data alterations.

WPA2 is an improved version of WPA, released in 2004. It utilizes the AES (Advanced Encryption Standard) encryption protocol, which is considered more secure than TKIP. AES uses symmetric block cipher encryption with 128-bit or 256-bit keys, which are robust enough to withstand brute-force attacks.

WPA3 (Wi-Fi Protected Access 3) is the latest encryption standard for WiFi networks. It was developed to replace WPA2, which was the most common encryption standard before the advent of WPA3. We will only mention it briefly in this book.

Currently, WPA2 is the most widely used WiFi security type, followed by WPA, with WEP gradually phasing out.

WPA3, on the other hand, is still relatively new, and its adoption is not yet widespread. It is important to note that WiFi security is constantly evolving, with new protocols and encryption algorithms being developed to counter increasingly sophisticated cyber threats.

Some network configurations can restrict client connections, such as using limited DHCP leases or configuring access restrictions based on MAC addresses.

Keep in mind that even with these limitations, an attacker who obtains your network key will still be able to capture and decrypt traffic on your network.

Indeed, once an attacker gains access to your network's security key, they can easily decrypt the traffic flowing through the network. This means they can intercept and read sensitive data such as login information, passwords, and personal data.

Chapter 1:
The Basics

Wi-Fi Protected Setup

WPS (Wi-Fi Protected Setup) is a configuration protocol for wireless networks designed to simplify the process of connecting devices to the WiFi network using an automatic pairing method.

WPS allows users to configure their wireless network by pressing a physical button on the router or entering an automatically generated 8-digit PIN code. This eliminates the need for users to manually enter network security information such as the SSID (network name) and security key.

However, this simplified configuration method has also created a significant security vulnerability. Attackers can use WPS attack tools to attempt to guess the 8-digit PIN code. If successful, the attacker can gain access to the wireless network and compromise data security.

There are two common types of WPS attacks:

Brute-force attack: The attacker tries all possible combinations of the PIN code until finding the correct one. This method can be time-consuming but can be automated using tools like Reaver or Bully.

Replay attack: The attacker captures the network traffic exchanged between the router and the device during the WPS connection attempt. Then, the attacker replays this network traffic to force the router to reveal the 8-digit PIN code.

To protect against WPS attacks, it is recommended to completely disable WPS on the router.

Chapter 1:
The Basics

The Human Factor

The human factor is a crucial element to consider when it comes to hacking.

The human factor is essential in hacking in general. Attackers often seek to exploit users' errors and weaknesses to gain access to target systems. Human errors, such as choosing weak passwords or clicking on phishing links, can often enable attackers to gain unauthorized access to systems.

However, users can also play an important role in preventing hacking attacks. Awareness of computer security is essential to help users understand the risks of computer security and best practices to protect against cyber attacks. Companies can provide training to their employees to help them understand the risks of computer security and best practices to protect against cyber attacks.

Computer security is a collective effort involving both users and companies. Users need to be aware of computer security risks and take steps to protect their systems and information, while companies need to implement strong security policies and provide tools and resources to help users protect against cyber attacks.

The human factor plays an important role in hacking, and it's not just about someone using the same old router since 2002 (in WEP, obviously). Examples of hacking show that even large companies and average users can be vulnerable to hacking attacks due to human errors.

Remember the massive hacking of Sony Pictures Entertainment in 2014? Hackers used phishing techniques to obtain login credentials from a Sony employee, which gave them unauthorized access to a vast network of computer systems. Therefore, human errors can play a crucial role in the computer security of large companies.

Here are a few examples of hacks on major companies where the human factor played a crucial role:

- **Phishing attack against John Podesta:** In 2016, John Podesta, the chairman of Hillary Clinton's presidential campaign, fell victim to a phishing attack. A fraudulent email was sent to his email account, prompting him to click on a malicious link that ultimately allowed hackers to access his account and steal sensitive information.

- **Target breach:** In 2013, hackers stole information from 110 million customers of the retail chain Target. The attack was initiated through the compromise of a third-party access account, which allowed hackers to access Target's payment systems.

- **Yahoo breach**: In 2013, hackers successfully stole personal information from over 3 billion Yahoo accounts. The attack was facilitated by the use of weak and easily guessable passwords, as well as inadequate security measures.

- **Democratic National Committee (DNC) breach in 2016:** During the 2016 U.S. presidential election, hackers conducted a series of attacks against the Democratic National Committee. They used phishing to obtain credentials from a DNC employee, enabling them to infiltrate the party's internal network and steal sensitive information.

- **WannaCry attack in 2017:** In 2017, the WannaCry ransomware infected over 200,000 computers in more than 150 countries, causing estimated losses of billions of dollars. The attack exploited a vulnerability in the Windows operating system, but its rapid spread was facilitated by many users failing to install security updates. Researchers also found a hardcoded email address in the ransomware code, suggesting that the human factor played a significant role in this attack as well.

- **In 1986, Kevin Mitnick successfully penetrated NASA's computer system** using social engineering techniques to gain access. He impersonated a Pacific Bell employee and requested system access from a NASA employee, pretending to be a security engineer from the telecommunications company.
(Mitnick was arrested for hacking NASA and many other companies in1995.)

Chapter 1:
The Basics

Types of Wireless Networks

There are several types of wireless networks, each with specific characteristics.

Wireless Local Area Networks (WLANs): These are wireless networks that allow device connectivity within a limited geographical area, such as a building, campus, or business. WLANs typically use the Wi-Fi protocol for wireless communication.

Wireless Metropolitan Area Networks (WMANs): These wireless networks cover a larger geographical area than WLANs, such as a city or region. Technologies used for WMANs include WiMAX and LTE.

Wireless Wide Area Networks (WWANs): These wireless networks cover an even larger geographical area than WMANs, such as 3G, 4G, and 5G mobile networks. WWANs are often used for mobile communication and long-distance data transmission.

Ad hoc networks: These are wireless networks created temporarily between multiple devices without requiring the use of a central access point. These networks can be used in emergency situations or to enable communication between remote devices.

Basic Tools for Wireless Hacking

There is a variety of tools for wireless hacking, ranging from packet analysis tools to password cracking tools. Here are some of the most commonly used tools:

- **Aircrack-ng:** A password cracking tool used to recover WEP and WPA keys. It can also be used for packet analysis functions.

- **Airplay-ng:** A tool used for generating network traffic to test the security of wireless networks. It can be used to launch Denial-of-Service (DoS) attacks and test network stability.

- **Airodump-ng:** A packet capture tool used to monitor network traffic on wireless networks. It can capture packets to obtain information about wireless networks, such as MAC addresses of access points and clients.

- **Tcpdump:** A packet analysis tool used to capture and display packets on a network. It can be used to capture and display packets on wireless networks.

- **Dnsmasq:** A lightweight DHCP and DNS server used to provide IP addresses and domain names to clients on a network. It can be used to launch DNS cache poisoning attacks.

- **Metasploit:** A vulnerability exploitation tool used to find and exploit vulnerabilities in wireless networks. It can be used to launch targeted attacks against wireless networks.

- **Arpspoof:** A tool used to redirect network traffic on a local network by sending forged ARP packets.

- **Nmap:** A network mapping tool used to discover hosts and services on a network. It can be used to scan wireless networks to gather information about access points and clients.

- **Dnsspoof:** A tool used to intercept and modify DNS traffic on a network, redirecting users to malicious sites or capturing sensitive information.

- **Hostapd:** A tool used to create a Wi-Fi access point.

Chapter 1:
The Basics

Fundamental Concepts

Wi-Fi network hacking has become increasingly common in recent years as more businesses and individuals use wireless networks to connect to the internet. If you're interested in Wi-Fi hacking, here are some key elements to know to get started.

Key Skills for Wi-Fi Hacking:

- A solid understanding of computer networks and their protocols, including Wi-Fi protocols such as 802.11a, 802.11b, 802.11g, and 802.11n.

- Understanding of Wi-Fi security protocols, such as WEP, WPA, and WPA2.

- Proficiency with Wi-Fi hacking tools such as Kali Linux, Aircrack-ng, Wireshark, Metasploit, and password cracking software suites.

- Ability to develop custom tools for specific attacks using programming languages like Bash, Python, PHP, and HTML.

- Skills in data analysis, including the ability to interpret results from network scans and traffic analyses.

Wi-Fi Hacking Techniques:

- Brute force attack (WPS): Testing all possible password (PIN) combinations until the correct one is found.

- Dictionary attack (4-way handshake): Using a list of words to try to guess the correct password.

- Replay attack: Capturing data packets sent between a wireless device and a Wi-Fi access point, then replaying them to access the wireless network without knowing the password.

- Rogue AP attack: Creating a fake Wi-Fi access point to trap users.

- Packet injection attack: Injecting malicious code into data packets to exploit vulnerabilities in the Wi-Fi network.

Chapter 1:
The Basics

Basic Concepts

Networks are key elements of modern connectivity. For hackers, a thorough understanding of these systems is essential for success in their activities.

Here's an overview of basic networking concepts for hackers:

IP Addressing: IP addressing is a system that identifies each device connected to a network by assigning it a unique address. Hackers need to understand how IP addressing works to identify different devices on a network and target them.

TCP Protocol: The Transmission Control Protocol (TCP) is a communication protocol that enables devices to communicate with each other over a network. It is a reliable protocol that ensures data is transmitted without errors and in order.

OSI Model: The OSI (Open Systems Interconnection) model is a reference model that describes the different layers of communication between devices on a network. Hackers need to understand the various layers of the OSI model to effectively manipulate data flowing through the network.

NAT: Network Address Translation (NAT) is a routing technique that allows multiple devices to connect to a single Internet access point. Hackers must understand how NAT works to bypass network restrictions and access devices that are normally out of reach.

Firewall: A firewall is a security device that controls incoming and outgoing network traffic. Hackers must be able to bypass firewalls to gain access to targeted networks.

DNS: The Domain Name System (DNS) is a system that translates domain names into IP addresses. Hackers need to understand how DNS works to manipulate DNS queries and redirect users to malicious websites.

Chapter 1:
The Basics

Basic Concepts

VLAN: Virtual Local Area Network (VLAN) is a logical network that allows segmentation of a physical network into multiple virtual networks. Hackers need to understand how VLAN segmentation works to access targeted network segments.

VPN: A Virtual Private Network (VPN) is a network that allows users to connect remotely to a private network via a public network.

Router: A router is a device that connects different networks and allows devices to communicate with each other over a network. Hackers need to understand how a router works to intercept and manipulate network traffic.

Port: A port is an access point to a computer or network service. Hackers need to understand how ports work to identify running services on a device and exploit them.

ICMP: Internet Control Message Protocol (ICMP) is a communication protocol that allows devices to control and diagnose network issues. Hackers need to understand how ICMP works to send falsified error messages and deceive network security devices.

UDP: User Datagram Protocol (UDP) is a transport layer communication protocol in the OSI (Open Systems Interconnection) model that allows datagrams to be sent across an IP network without establishing a prior connection between the two endpoints. Unlike TCP, which ensures data delivery and error correction by establishing a connection before sending data, UDP is a connectionless protocol that does not guarantee data delivery, the order of reception, or data integrity.

POSIX: POSIX commands are system commands available in Unix and Unix-like environments.

MITM: MITM stands for "Man In The Middle," which refers to an attack where an attacker intercepts communications between two legitimate parties.

Chapter 1:
The Basics

Basic Concepts

Hackers also need programming skills to succeed in their activities. Here are some programming languages commonly used by hackers:

Bash: Bash is a scripting language used for task automation on Unix and Linux systems. Hackers often use Bash to create scripts that automate repetitive tasks, such as gathering information about a network.

Python: Python is a widely used interpreted programming language for script development, web applications, and data processing applications. Hackers frequently use Python to write scripts that automate complex tasks, such as hacking into systems.

PHP: PHP is a server-side scripting language commonly used for creating dynamic and interactive websites. Hackers often use PHP for exploiting security vulnerabilities in web applications.

C/C++: C and C++ are low-level programming languages commonly used for system software development and device drivers. Intermediate-level hackers often use these languages to create security exploits and malware.

Ruby: Ruby is an interpreted programming language commonly used for script and web application development. Intermediate-level hackers often use Ruby to create vulnerability analysis tools and security exploit scripts.

Java: Java is an object-oriented programming language commonly used for developing applications for platforms such as Android. Intermediate-level hackers often use Java to create malware and hacking tools for Android platforms.

JavaScript: JavaScript is a scripting language primarily used for client-side web development. Hackers often use JavaScript to exploit web application vulnerabilities, manipulate web pages dynamically, and conduct cross-site scripting (XSS) attacks.

HTML: HTML (HyperText Markup Language) is the standard markup language for creating web pages and web applications. While not a programming language, hackers often manipulate HTML to inject malicious code, such as phishing forms or JavaScript payloads, into web pages to exploit vulnerabilities.

Chapter 1:
The Basics

Basic Concepts

Different Levels of Programming Languages:

Low-level languages: Low-level languages are very close to machine language. They use a very simple syntax and are often difficult to read and write for programmers. Examples of low-level languages include assembly language and machine language.

Intermediate-level languages: Intermediate-level languages are designed to be more user-friendly than low-level languages while offering performance close to that of low-level languages. They are typically compiled and require knowledge of memory and processor architecture concepts. Examples of intermediate-level languages include C and C++.

High-level languages: High-level languages are designed to be more user-friendly than intermediate-level languages. They are often interpreted and are designed to be easier to learn and use. Examples of high-level languages include Python, Ruby, and Java.

Very high-level languages: Very high-level languages are programming languages that are even more user-friendly than high-level languages. They are often used for productivity applications and rapid application development (RAD). Examples of very high-level languages include Visual Basic, JavaScript, and PHP.

It is worth noting that the distinction between different levels of languages is not always clear-cut, as there are often languages that borrow features from different levels.

A compiled language is a programming language whose source code is translated into executable binary code before execution. The compiler analyzes the entire source code and generates an executable file optimized for the target system. The resulting code can be executed directly on the target system without needing an interpreter or compiler.

An interpreted language is a programming language whose source code is executed directly without needing to be compiled into machine code. An interpreter analyzes each instruction of the source code and translates it into machine code on-the-fly. Interpreted languages are often more flexible and portable than compiled languages, as the same source code can be executed on different systems without requiring prior compilation.

Chapter 1:
The Basics

Basic Concepts

IP Addressing is a system used to identify each device connected to a network by assigning it a unique address. This address is composed of a series of binary numbers, but for easier human comprehension, it is typically displayed in decimal format and separated into four octets.

There are two versions of IP addressing: IPv4 and IPv6.

IPv4 uses 32-bit addresses, allowing up to 4.3 billion devices to be addressed. IPv6, which uses 128-bit addresses, capable of addressing an astronomical number of devices.

There are five classes of IP addresses: A, B, C, D, and E.

Class A: Class A addresses are used for large networks. The first octet of the address is reserved for the network, and the remaining three octets are used to identify devices on the network. Class A addresses range from 1.0.0.0 to 126.0.0.0, with one address reserved for loopback (127.0.0.0).

Class B: Class B addresses are used for medium-sized networks. The first two octets of the address are reserved for the network, and the remaining two octets are used to identify devices on the network. Class B addresses range from 128.0.0.0 to 191.255.0.0.

Class C: Class C addresses are used for small networks. The first three octets of the address are reserved for the network, and the last octet is used to identify devices on the network. Class C addresses range from 192.0.0.0 to 223.255.255.0.

Class D: Class D addresses are used for multicast data transmission to a group of devices. Class D addresses range from 224.0.0.0 to 239.255.255.255.

Class E: Class E addresses are reserved for experimental use and are not used to identify devices on a network. Class E addresses range from 240.0.0.0 to 255.255.255.255.

It should be noted that Class A, B, and C addresses are the most commonly used for networks. Class D and E addresses are reserved for special use and are not used to identify devices on a network.

Chapter 1:
The Basics

Basic Concepts

The Internet Protocol (IP) is a communication protocol that enables devices to communicate with each other over an IP network. It is responsible for routing data packets across the network using unique IP addresses to identify each device.

IP operates at the network layer of the **OSI model** and is responsible for routing data packets across networks. It uses an IP address to identify each device on the network and determine the route for data delivery.

It is designed to work on heterogeneous networks, meaning networks that can have different types of devices and technologies. It is also designed to be scalable, so it can support new types of devices and technologies as they emerge.

The Internet Protocol has two main versions: IPv4 and IPv6.

IPv4 is the most widely used version

The Internet Protocol works by breaking down data into small packets, adding a destination address (IP address) to each packet, and then sending these packets across the network.

Each device connected to a network has a unique IP address, which is used to identify the device when it communicates with other devices on the network. When a device sends data to another device, it breaks the data into appropriately sized packets, adds the destination IP address to each packet, and then sends the packets across the network. Routers examine the destination IP address of each packet they receive and then decide which port to forward the packet to so it reaches its destination.

Regarding hacking, the Internet Protocol is often targeted in attacks, including Denial of Service (DoS) attacks.

Hackers can also use techniques such as IP address spoofing to falsify the source IP address of a data packet, which can be used to mask their identity or deceive the packet's recipient.

It is also possible to exploit vulnerabilities in the implementation of the Internet Protocol to compromise devices on a network.

Chapter 1:
The Basics

Basic Concepts

TCP (Transmission Control Protocol) is a reliable, connection-oriented communication protocol used to ensure error-free data transmission between computers on a network.

It operates at the transport layer of the **OSI model** and uses port numbers to identify applications running on connected machines.

TCP employs a flow control and error recovery system to ensure that all data is transmitted correctly. When one computer sends data to another, TCP breaks down the data into smaller segments and adds headers to each segment indicating the destination address, source address, sequence numbers, acknowledgments (ACKs), and other crucial information.

TCP uses a sequence numbering system to ensure that all data is transmitted in the correct order. Each segment sent is numbered with a unique sequence number, and the receiver sends back an acknowledgment (ACK) for each received segment. If a segment is not received correctly, TCP uses an error recovery system to request retransmission of that segment.

In addition to error recovery and flow control, TCP also includes mechanisms to manage network congestion. If network traffic is too high, TCP reduces the data transmission rate to prevent congestion.

TCP is widely used in applications that require reliable and error-free communication, such as email, file transfer, and web browsing.

However, TCP's flow control and error recovery system can lead to increased latency, making it less suitable for applications that require fast and real-time data transmission.

Chapter 1:
The Basics

Basic Concepts

The OSI (Open Systems Interconnection) model is a reference model for communications between computers or devices on a network. It consists of seven layers, each with a specific role in handling data exchanged between devices.

Here is a brief description of each of the seven layers of the OSI model:

- **Physical Layer:** This layer defines the hardware specifications of the network, such as cable types and connection interfaces.

- **Data Link Layer:** This layer handles the transmission of data between devices on the same physical network using MAC addresses.

- **Network Layer:** This layer manages the routing of data between different networks using IP addresses.

- **Transport Layer**: This layer manages the reliable transmission of data between applications on different devices using protocols such as TCP or UDP.

- **Session Layer:** This layer establishes, manages, and terminates sessions between applications on devices.

- **Presentation Layer:** This layer manages the representation of data exchanged between applications by handling data conversion into a format understandable by applications.

- **Application Layer:** This layer contains applications that access the network, such as web browsers, email clients, etc.

Each layer of the OSI model has specific functions and associated protocols. Network devices must be compatible with the different layers of the OSI model to communicate with each other effectively.

Chapter 1:
The Basics

Basic Concepts

The OSI Model (Open Systems Interconnection)

Here are two examples to illustrate how the OSI layers work:

When you type a URL into your web browser and press "Enter," the browser sends an HTTP request to a remote web server. The request passes through all OSI layers to reach its destination.

Here's how it works:

Layer 7 (Application): Your browser creates the HTTP request.

Layer 6 (Presentation): The HTTP request is converted into a standardized data format.

Layer 5 (Session): A session is established between the browser and the remote web server to ensure error-free communication.

Layer 4 (Transport): The HTTP request is segmented into appropriately sized segments for transport over the network.

Layer 3 (Network): The segments are encapsulated into IP packets to be sent over the network.

Layer 2 (Data Link): IP packets are encapsulated into frames to be sent over the network.

Layer 1 (Physical): Frames are transmitted over the network via electrical or optical signals.

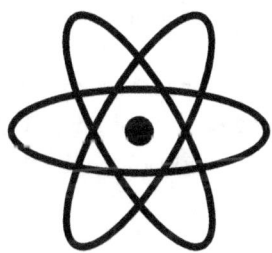

Chapter 1:
The Basics

Basic Concepts

The OSI Model (Open Systems Interconnection)

Connecting to Wi-Fi through OSI Layers:

Physical Layer: When you enable Wi-Fi on your device, it sends a radio frequency (RF) signal that is transmitted through the air to the Wi-Fi access point. This RF signal constitutes the physical layer.

Data Link Layer: The Wi-Fi access point receives the RF signal and uses the data link layer to transmit authentication information to your device. This layer ensures that data is transmitted without errors and that data packets are correctly ordered.

Network Layer: Once your device is connected to the Wi-Fi access point, it uses the network layer to obtain an IP address. An IP address is a unique identifier that allows your device to communicate on the network. This layer also facilitates the creation of IP data packets.

Transport Layer: The transport layer is responsible for managing end-to-end connections between applications. In the case of Wi-Fi, this layer handles the transmission of IP packets between your device and the Wi-Fi access point.

Session Layer: The session layer is responsible for opening, managing, and closing sessions between applications. In the context of Wi-Fi, this layer can be used to establish a secure session for transmitting sensitive data.

Presentation Layer: The presentation layer is responsible for data representation for applications. In the case of Wi-Fi, this layer ensures compatibility between different data formats.

Application Layer: Finally, the application layer is responsible for the applications themselves. In the context of Wi-Fi, this could include applications such as web browsers or messaging applications.

Chapter 1:
The Basics

Basic Concepts

Network Address Translation (NAT) is a process used to translate IP addresses to connect computers from a local network to the Internet. NAT is typically used when the IP address of the local network is not routable on the Internet, meaning it cannot be used to communicate with other networks.

It works by replacing the source IP address of a packet with a public IP address before it is sent over the Internet. When a response is received for the packet, NAT replaces the public IP address with the local IP address and forwards the packet back to the original device.

NAT can be implemented in various ways, but one of the most common methods is NAT with private IP address.

Example to illustrate Network Address Translation:

Let's assume a company has an internal network with several computers that need to access the Internet. The company uses a single public IP address for its Internet access provided by its Internet Service Provider (ISP).

To allow all computers to connect to the Internet, a router is used to translate the private IP addresses of the computers into a single public IP address.

When a computer in the company sends a request to a web server on the Internet, the source IP address of the computer is the private IP address assigned to it by the router.

When the web server's response is sent back to the computer, it is sent to the company's public IP address. The router receives the response and translates it into a private IP address corresponding to the computer that initially sent the request.

This allows the computer to access the requested content on the Internet without disclosing its private IP address outside of the company.

Therefore, NAT is an essential mechanism to allow multiple computers to access the Internet using a single public IP address.

Chapter 1:
The Basics

Basic Concepts

A firewall is a security device that filters incoming and outgoing network traffic of a computer network. It can be hardware-based or software-based and is used to prevent malicious attacks such as intrusions, viruses, and malware.

The firewall operates by applying a set of rules or policies to determine whether traffic should be allowed or blocked. These rules can be based on IP addresses, ports, protocols, traffic types, etc. *For example, the firewall can be configured to allow HTTP traffic (port 80) but block SMTP traffic (port 25).*

There are different types of firewalls, such as packet-filtering firewalls, circuit-level gateways, application-layer firewalls, etc. Each type uses different techniques to filter network traffic.

The firewall is a crucial element of computer security and is often used in combination with other security technologies such as antivirus, antispam, etc.

An example of configuring a firewall on Linux could be using the iptables command to block unauthorized incoming connections on a specific port.

For instance, to block incoming connections on port 22 (used by SSH), you can use the following command:

"sudo iptables -A INPUT -p tcp --dport 22 -j DROP"

Chapter 1:
The Basics

Basic Concepts

The Domain Name System (DNS) has existed since the 1980s. It is a system that translates domain names (such as google.com) into IP addresses (such as 172.217.0.46).

When you enter a website's address into your browser, your computer sends a request for domain name resolution to a DNS server. This server then looks up the IP address corresponding to the requested domain name and returns this information to the user's computer. This IP address is then used to establish a connection with the website.

DNS is a distributed system, which means it uses many different servers to respond to domain name resolution requests. These servers are organized in a hierarchy, with root servers at the top, followed by top-level domain servers, second-level domain servers, and so on.

DNS is essential for the operation of the Internet because it allows users to connect to websites using easy-to-remember domain names rather than using numerical IP addresses, which are difficult to memorize. Additionally, DNS facilitates communication between various online services, such as mail servers and instant messaging servers, by allowing them to identify each other using domain names.

The process of resolving domain names to IP addresses involves several steps:

- The DNS client sends a domain name resolution request to its local DNS server.
- If the local DNS server already has the corresponding IP address cached, it returns it to the DNS client.
- Otherwise, the local DNS server sends a request to the root DNS server to obtain the IP address of the top-level domain DNS server (.com, .org, .net, etc.) corresponding to the requested domain name.
- The root DNS server returns the IP address of the top-level domain DNS server to the local DNS server.
- The local DNS server then sends a request to the top-level domain DNS server to obtain the IP address of the second-level domain server (for example, google.com).
- The top-level domain DNS server returns the IP address of the second-level domain server to the local DNS server.
- Finally, the local DNS server sends a request to the second-level domain DNS server to obtain the IP address corresponding to the requested domain name.
- The second-level domain DNS server returns the corresponding IP address to the local DNS server, which then returns it to the DNS client.

The domain name resolution process may seem complex, but It actually happens very quickly, typically within milliseconds. It is crucial for enabling users to access websites and online services using easy-to-remember domain names rather than numerical IP addresses.

Chapter 1:
The Basics

Basic Concepts

DNS (Domain Name System)

In the context of "DNS Spoofing" or "DNS cache poisoning" attacks, an attacker modifies DNS records to redirect users to malicious sites.

This can allow the attacker to steal sensitive information such as login credentials or install malware on the victim's system. Attackers can also use DNS to bypass security measures by using domain names that appear legitimate but point to malicious IP addresses.

DNS zone transfer is a process in which an authoritative name server shares its DNS zone database with another name server. This allows two name servers to remain synchronized with the same DNS zone information.

Regarding hacking, DNS zone transfer can be used to retrieve sensitive information about an organization, such as internal IP addresses, hostnames, and service records. This can help an attacker map out the organization's network and plan targeted attacks.

Therefore, it is important for DNS server administrators to restrict access to DNS zone transfer only to authorized name servers.

Chapter 1:
The Basics

Basic Concepts

A VLAN (Virtual Local Area Network) is a logical network that allows devices to be grouped based on defined criteria, independent of their physical location within the network. VLANs are used to segment a network into multiple virtual sub-networks, each with its own security and management rules.

To understand how VLANs work, it's important to understand the role of switches in a network. Switches are devices that connect multiple devices together, forwarding data packets between different ports. Switches can also use VLANs to isolate certain ports or groups of ports from the rest of the network. Each VLAN is identified by a VLAN ID, which is a number ranging from 1 to 4094. Data packets traveling on the network are tagged with a VLAN tag that indicates which VLAN they belong to. Switches use these VLAN tags to route data packets to the appropriate devices.

VLANs can be defined in various ways:

Port-based VLANs are the most common: each port on the switch is associated with a specific VLAN.

MAC address-based VLANs are also possible: devices are associated with a VLAN based on their MAC address.

VLANs allow a network to be segmented into multiple virtual sub-networks, each with its own security and management rules. The benefits of VLANs are numerous: they help reduce network traffic, isolate groups of devices, limit broadcast of data packets, and facilitate network management.

However, setting up VLANs can be complex, especially when defining security rules and management policies. Therefore, careful planning is essential when implementing VLANs, ensuring that switches and network devices are compatible with this technology.

Chapter 1:
The Basics

Basic Concepts

A VPN (Virtual Private Network) is a virtual private network that securely connects computers and remote networks over the Internet. The VPN creates an encrypted tunnel between the two connection points, so that all data flowing through the network is encrypted and cannot be intercepted by malicious third parties.

The VPN operates by encapsulating data into encrypted packets that are then transmitted over the Internet. When the data reaches its destination, it is decrypted and unpacked. This helps protect sensitive data such as passwords, credit card information, and confidential business data from hackers and other malicious individuals.

There are two main types of VPN:

Remote Access VPN: This type of VPN allows an individual user to securely connect to a remote network. The user can access resources on the remote network, such as files, printers, or applications, as if they were physically present on the network.

Site-to-Site VPN: This type of VPN connects two separate networks, such as two offices of a company, securely. Data is transmitted between the two networks via the VPN tunnel, enabling employees from each office to access resources from the other office.

VPNs can also be configured to use different security protocols such as PPTP (Point-to-Point Tunneling Protocol), L2TP (Layer 2 Tunneling Protocol), and OpenVPN. These protocols are used to establish and manage the VPN connection, as well as to encrypt the data passing through it.

The VPN is an essential security tool for businesses and individual users who want to protect their data against cyberattacks and other online threats. It creates a secure virtual private network that connects computers and remote networks over the Internet, ensuring that all data transmitted through it is encrypted and protected from hackers and other malicious individuals.

Chapter 1:
The Basics

Basic Concepts

A router is a network device used to interconnect multiple computer networks, such as local area networks (LANs) and wide area networks (WANs). Its main role is to direct traffic between different networks using routing tables to determine the best path for routing data packets.

The router operates at Layer 3 of the OSI model, known as the OSI (Open Systems Interconnection) reference model.

At Layer 3, the protocol used is the Internet Protocol (IP), which facilitates the transmission of data packets from one network to another.

A router typically has at least two network interfaces, one for each network it connects. Data packets entering the router are analyzed to determine their destination and the best path to route them to their destination.

Hacking often involves manipulating or bypassing a router's routing rules to gain unauthorized access to networks or devices. Hackers may use techniques such as route hijacking or IP address spoofing to deceive the router and route their traffic to networks they are not authorized to access.

Routers can also be targeted for hacking to take control of the network or to perform denial of service (DDoS) attacks by saturating incoming or outgoing network traffic.

Therefore, router security is a major concern for network administrators and cybersecurity experts. Best security practices include regularly updating router firmware, configuring strong passwords, and implementing measures to protect against denial of service attacks.

Chapter 1:
The Basics

Basic Concepts

Ports are virtual channels used for communication between different programs or devices on a computer network. Each network communication is associated with a port number that identifies the process or application sending or receiving the data.

Port numbers are integers ranging from 0 to 65535.

There are two types of ports Well-known ports and ephemeral ports.:

- **Well-known ports are numbered from 0 to 1023** and are reserved for specific applications or services, such as port 80 for HTTP requests or port 22 for SSH connections.

- **Ephemeral ports are numbered from 1024 to 65535** and are used for temporary connections between applications or devices. These ports are often automatically generated by operating systems and are released once the communication is finished.

While well-known ports are typically reserved for specific applications, it is technically possible to launch any service on any port.

The use of ports is essential for communication between different devices on a network. Communication protocols such as TCP or UDP use port numbers to route data to the appropriate applications.

In terms of cybersecurity, ports can be used to detect vulnerabilities or to block access to specific applications or services.

Hackers can also use port scanning techniques to identify active services on a system and attempt to exploit known vulnerabilities associated with those services.

Ultimately, ports are essential virtual communication channels for communication between applications or devices on a network, and their management can have a significant impact on cybersecurity.

Chapter 1:
The Basics

Basic Concepts

Here is a list of the most well-known ports and their usage:

TCP:

- 20: FTP (File Transfer Protocol) - data
- 21: FTP (File Transfer Protocol) - command
- 22: SSH (Secure Shell)
- 23: Telnet
- 25: SMTP (Simple Mail Transfer Protocol)
- 53: DNS (Domain Name System)
- 80: HTTP (Hypertext Transfer Protocol)
- 110: POP3 (Post Office Protocol version 3)
- 143: IMAP (Internet Message Access Protocol)
- 443: HTTPS (HTTP over SSL/TLS)
- 3389: RDP (Remote Desktop Protocol)
- 8080: HTTP alternate (often used as proxy or for web servers in development)
- 465/TCP: SMTPS (SMTP Secure)
- 514/UDP: syslog (System Logging Protocol)
- 636/TCP: LDAPS (LDAP Secure)
- 993/TCP: IMAPS (IMAP Secure)
- 995/TCP: POP3S (POP3 Secure)
- 1433/TCP: Microsoft SQL Server
- 3306/TCP: MySQL

UDP:

- 53: DNS (Domain Name System)
- 67: DHCP (Dynamic Host Configuration Protocol) - server
- 68: DHCP (Dynamic Host Configuration Protocol) - client
- 69: TFTP (Trivial File Transfer Protocol)
- 123: NTP (Network Time Protocol)
- 161: SNMP (Simple Network Management Protocol)
- 500: IPSec (Internet Protocol Security)
- 514: syslog (used for system logs)
- 1900: SSDP (Simple Service Discovery Protocol)
- 5353: mDNS (multicast DNS)

Chapter 1:
The Basics

Basic Concepts

ICMP (Internet Control Message Protocol) is a network layer protocol used to communicate control and error messages between devices on an IP network.

It allows routers and other network devices to communicate diagnostic information to other devices on the network.

ICMP is a Layer 3 protocol that uses messages to transmit control information. ICMP messages are encapsulated within IP packets and are transmitted between routers and other network devices.

ICMP messages serve various functions, such as signaling routing errors, diagnosing network connectivity, monitoring quality of service, and managing network traffic. Some commonly used ICMP messages include:

- Echo Request and Echo Reply: These messages are used to test connectivity between two devices. When a device sends an Echo Request to another device, the latter must respond with an Echo Reply.
-
- Destination Unreachable: This message is used to indicate that a packet could not be delivered to its destination. This may be due to routing errors or other conditions preventing packet delivery.
-
- Time Exceeded: This message is used to indicate that a packet could not reach its destination within a reasonable time frame. This could be due to network congestion or routing errors.
-
- Redirect: This message is used by a router to inform a device on the network how to reach a destination more efficiently.
-
- Router Advertisement and Router Solicitation: These messages are used to announce the presence of a router on the network and to obtain routing information.

ICMP messages are used for various maintenance and diagnostic tasks on an IP network. However, like all network protocols, they can also be exploited for malicious purposes. Hackers may use forged ICMP messages to launch denial-of-service attacks or to conceal their presence on a network. Therefore, it is important for network administrators to monitor ICMP traffic and take measures to prevent potential attacks.

Chapter 1:
The Basics

Basic Concepts

UDP (User Datagram Protocol) is a data transport protocol in computer networks. Unlike TCP, it does not provide flow control, error checking, or retransmission of lost packets. UDP is therefore faster than TCP but less reliable.

UDP operates simply: the protocol encapsulates the data to be transmitted into a UDP datagram, which includes the IP addresses of the sender and receiver, as well as source and destination port numbers. Once the datagram is created, it is sent over the network without any additional control.

The main advantage of UDP is its speed because there is no waiting time for error checking or retransmission of lost packets. This makes it suitable for real-time applications such as Voice over IP (VoIP) and online gaming.

However, this also means that data transmitted via UDP can be lost or arrive out of order, which can cause quality issues for some applications.

The User Datagram Protocol (UDP) can be used in the realm of hacking, including for the following actions:

- **Denial of Service (DoS) and Distributed Denial of Service (DDoS) attacks:** Attackers can use UDP to send a large number of UDP packets to a target, which can overload the network and render services unavailable.

- **Port scanning:** Port scanning tools, such as Nmap, can use UDP to detect open ports on a target.

- **DNS amplification attacks:** Attackers can use misconfigured DNS servers to send large UDP packets to a target, using the DNS server's IP address as the source address. This technique can amplify the power of the attack and cause significant damage.

- **UDP flood attacks:** Attackers can send a large number of UDP packets to a target without needing to establish a prior connection, with the aim of saturating it.

- **Packet injection:** Attackers can inject malicious UDP packets into a network traffic stream to disrupt the operation of target systems or exploit vulnerabilities.

It is important to note that UDP itself is not malicious; rather, it is the way it is used for malicious purposes.

Chapter 1:
The Basics

Basic Concepts

POSIX commands are system commands available in Unix and Unix-like environments. These commands are defined by POSIX (Portable Operating System Interface) standards, which aim to facilitate software portability across different operating systems. POSIX commands are therefore available on most Unix and Unix-like systems, such as Linux, macOS, FreeBSD, etc.

Here are some examples of commonly used POSIX commands:

- **cd:** change directory
- **ls**: list directory contents
- **cat:** concatenate and display files
- **echo:** display text on the screen
- **cp:** copy files
- **mv**: move files or directories
- **rm**: remove files or directories
- **mkdir:** make directories
- **rmdir**: remove empty directories
- **chmod:** change file or directory permissions
- **chown:** change file or directory owner and group
- **grep:** search text within files
- **awk:** pattern scanning and processing language
- **sed**: stream editor for filtering and transforming text
- **od:** display file content in octal, hexadecimal, or other formats
- **paste:** merge lines of multiple files
- **pwd:** print working directory
- **sleep:** suspend execution for a specified time
- **sort:** sort lines of text files
- **split:** split a file into pieces

There are many other POSIX commands available, but these are among the most commonly used ones.

Chapter 1:
The Basics

Basic Concepts

There are several POSIX commands that are useful for hacking and security activities. Here are some examples:

- **ping:** a command that sends ICMP packets to an IP address to test network connectivity.
- **ifconfig:** a command used to configure network interfaces on a system.
- **route**: a command used to manipulate the system's routing table to define specific routes.
- **arp:** a command used to view and manipulate the ARP table, which maps IP addresses to MAC addresses.
- **iptables**: a command used to configure the netfilter firewall in the Linux kernel.
- **dig:** a command used to retrieve DNS information such as A, MX, and TXT records.
- **host:** a command used to resolve hostnames to IP addresses and vice versa.
- **ssh:** a command used to securely connect to a remote system and execute commands there.
- **scp:** a command used to securely copy files between systems via SSH.
- **netstat:** a command used to display current network connections, open ports, network statistics, etc.
- **traceroute:** a command used to trace the path of packets across a network to their destination.
- **nslookup:** a command used to query a DNS server for information about domain names.
- **whois:** a command used to retrieve information about domain owners, IP addresses, and networks.
- **curl:** a command used to retrieve resources from web servers via HTTP, HTTPS, FTP, etc.
- **wget:** a command used to download files from web servers via HTTP, HTTPS, and FTP.

Some of these commands may not be installed by default on all POSIX systems and may require additional installation.

There are of course many other POSIX commands that can be useful for hacking and security activities, but these are among the most commonly used ones.

Chapter 1:
The Basics

The Principle of Man-in-the-Middle (MITM) Attacks

Man-in-the-Middle (MITM) attacks are a common method of hacking wireless networks.
The principle of a MITM attack is to allow an attacker to position themselves between two legitimate parties who are communicating, in order to monitor and intercept their communication.

MITM attacks involve intercepting communications between two parties and relaying this information in real-time to each party, allowing the attacker to act as an intermediary. **Thus, the attacker can eavesdrop, modify, or even inject data into the communication.**

MITM attacks are particularly dangerous for wireless networks because users are not always able to detect that they are communicating with an attacker rather than the legitimate party.

There are several types of MITM attacks, including:

- **Packet Sniffing Attacks:** These attacks involve intercepting packets that are transmitted between two parties on a network and analyzing or modifying them before forwarding them to their destination. This allows the attacker to retrieve sensitive information such as usernames or passwords.

- **Packet Injection Attacks:** These attacks involve inserting malicious packets into the network data stream. The packets may contain malware or commands that allow the attacker to take control of the target system.

- **Relay Attacks:** These attacks involve intercepting traffic between two parties on a network and relaying it to another system without the involved parties realizing it. This can allow the attacker to gain control of a system without the user noticing that something is wrong.

- **Redirection Attacks:** These attacks involve redirecting network traffic to a destination other than the one intended by the user. This can allow the attacker to retrieve sensitive information such as usernames or passwords.

Chapter 1:
The Basics

Principle of MITM Attacks

Spoofing is a commonly used technique in MITM attacks. It involves impersonating a user or system to deceive other users and gain access to sensitive data.

There are several types of spoofing, including:

- **ARP spoofing** involves falsifying ARP tables on the network to redirect traffic to an attacker's system, allowing them to intercept packets and access data.

- **DNS spoofing** involves falsifying DNS records to redirect traffic to a malicious website controlled by the attacker (as used in the previous chapter to redirect the client to our fake page).

- **TCP packet spoofing** involves falsifying TCP packet headers to impersonate a system and interfere with communication between two systems.

- **SSL certificate spoofing** involves creating a fraudulent SSL certificate to deceive users into believing they are communicating with a legitimate secure website, when in fact they are communicating with a malicious website controlled by the attacker.

ARP and DNS spoofing can also be used together to conduct a phishing attack on the network.

Note that in the case of our rogue AP seen earlier, once the attacker successfully impersonates the legitimate AP and a client connects to it, they simply need to modify the DNS configuration to launch a phishing attack (since they are already in a MITM position as the client's router).

Chapter 1:
The Basics

Here are some examples of attacks using spoofing:

- **Man-in-the-Middle (MITM) Attack:** This attack involves intercepting communication between two systems to eavesdrop or inject malicious data. MITM is often performed using ARP spoofing or falsified TCP packets.

- **Phishing Attack by Spoofing:** This attack involves sending fraudulent emails or messages using the email address of a trusted company or individual. Users are often prompted to click on a link or download an attachment that infects their system or divulges sensitive information.

- **Session Hijacking Attack:** This attack involves impersonating a logged-in user on a website by capturing their login session. The attacker can then use this session to access the user's data or functionality, or even take control of their account.

- **DNS Cache Poisoning Attack:** This attack involves falsifying DNS records on a domain name server to redirect traffic to a malicious website controlled by the attacker.

- **Route Poisoning Attack:** This attack involves falsifying routing tables on a router to redirect traffic to an attacker's system. This technique is often used in Distributed Denial of Service (DDoS) attacks.

- **Rogue Access Point Attack (or Evil Twin):** This attack involves creating a fraudulent Wi-Fi access point to deceive users into thinking they are connecting to a legitimate Wi-Fi network. The attacker can then intercept their network traffic or redirect them to malicious websites.

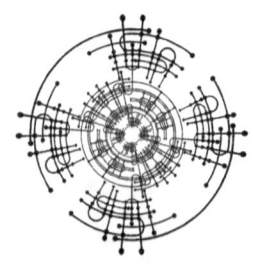

Chapter 1: The Basics

Here is a list of the main MITM tools:

- **Ettercap:** A packet sniffer and interception tool that also enables MITM attacks.
- **SSLStrip:** A tool that circumvents SSL/TLS security on websites by forcing connections to HTTP.
- **Bettercap:** A comprehensive MITM tool that captures and analyzes network traffic, injects packets, and performs MITM attacks.
- **Arpspoof:** An ARP spoofing tool that redirects traffic to an attacker's machine for packet interception.
- **Dsniff:** A suite of packet sniffing tools that capture passwords, login sessions, and other sensitive data.
- **MITMProxy**: An HTTP/HTTPS proxy that captures and modifies requests and responses for MITM attacks.
- **EvilGrade:** A tool that performs malicious update attacks to install malware on vulnerable machines.

These tools can be used to carry out MITM attacks. It is important to emphasize that their use must be ethical and legal, with the authorization of the owners of the targeted networks and systems.

MITM attack tools are often used to place an attacker in the so-called man-in-the-middle situation, which allows the attacker to monitor and intercept communications between two parties without their knowledge.

However, attackers do not limit themselves to this technique alone. They may also use sniffing tools to intercept and analyze data packets traveling over the network to extract sensitive information such as passwords or personal data.

Packet injection is also a common technique in MITM attacks, allowing the attacker to send malicious packets over the network to introduce malicious code, alter data, or disrupt system functionality. Social engineering techniques may also be used to obtain sensitive information from users.

Chapter 1: The Basics

Here are some defense and countermeasure tools against MITM attacks:

- **HTTPS Everywhere: A** browser extension that encrypts HTTPS connections to prevent man-in-the-middle attacks.
- **DNSSEC:** A security extension for the DNS protocol that verifies the authenticity of DNS responses, preventing MITM attacks.
- **Valid SSL Certificates:** Using valid SSL certificates issued by a recognized certificate authority ensures the authenticity of the website and prevents MITM attacks.
- **Virtual Private Networks (VPNs):** VPNs use encryption protocols to establish secure connections between remote computers, thereby preventing MITM attacks.
- **Firewall:** A firewall can be used to block malicious network traffic and prevent MITM attacks.
- **Arpwatch:** A network monitoring tool that detects ARP spoofing attacks.
- **Wireshark:** A network traffic analysis tool that can be used to detect MITM attacks.
- **Nmap:** A network discovery tool that can be used to detect unauthorized hosts on a network.
- **Port Sentry:** A tool that monitors open ports and sends alerts when an unauthorized port is used.

It is important to note that these tools are not exhaustive, and it is recommended to use multiple tools and defense techniques to enhance the security of a network against MITM attacks.

Here are some scenario ideas to help you learn the basics of hacking and networking:

- **Set Up a Home Network with a Firewall:** Create a home network with a firewall and filtering rules to protect your network from attacks.
- **Configure a Mail Server:** Set up a mail server and test its security by simulating phishing attacks.
- **Network Protection System:** Implement a network protection system using packet filtering tools such as iptables or pfSense.
- **Vulnerable Virtual Machine:** Set up a vulnerable virtual machine and attempt to exploit it using known exploits, but only for educational purposes.
- **Network Security Testing Environment:** Create a testing environment to assess network security using packet sniffing tools like Wireshark to analyze network traffic.

If you are an intermediate-level hacker, it is recommended to move on to more advanced and complex scenarios. Here are some ideas to continue improving your hacking skills:

- **Session Cookie Hijacking:** Set up a testing environment and attempt to hijack session cookies to gain unauthorized access to user accounts.
- **Web Server and SQL Injection Tests:** Configure a web server and conduct SQL injection tests to try to retrieve database information.
- **Network Traffic Interception:** Use tools like Wireshark or tcpdump to intercept and analyze network traffic, aiming to find sensitive information such as passwords.
- **Honeypot or Rogue AP Setup:** Implement a honeypot or rogue access point to attract attackers and analyze their attack methods.
- **Bypass Firewall:** Configure a firewall and try to bypass it using various attack techniques such as packet injection or tunneling.
- **Advanced Phishing Tests:** Conduct advanced phishing tests using tools like Gophish to simulate spear-phishing attacks.
- **Vulnerability Analysis with Metasploit:** Use vulnerability analysis tools like Metasploit to detect and exploit security flaws in a system.
- **Man-in-the-Middle Attacks:** Set up a testing environment and perform man-in-the-middle attacks.
- **VPN Compromise:** Configure a virtual private network (VPN) and attempt to compromise it using various attack techniques.

Chapter 2:
Dictionary Attack

Chapter 2:
Dictionary Attack

The Basics of Dictionary Attacks

Dictionary attacks are a commonly used method by hackers to attempt to guess passwords.

This technique involves using a list of common words or combinations of words and numbers to try to guess the correct password. Unlike a brute force attack, which tries all possible combinations, a dictionary attack focuses on the most common words and combinations of words.

Therefore, this method can be faster and more efficient than a brute force attack, but it is also limited to the words and combinations of words contained in the dictionary.

Here are the strengths and weaknesses of the dictionary attack on WPA/WPA2 Wi-Fi:

Strengths:

- **Effective for Weak and Common Passwords:** It works well against weak and commonly used passwords.
- **Easy to Implement:** Can be implemented easily with a basic Linux setup.
- **Vulnerability** in WPA/WPA2 Encryption: WPA/WPA2 encryption is vulnerable to dictionary attacks because it uses a relatively weak key derivation function called PBKDF2.

Weaknesses:

- **Ineffective for Strong Passwords:** Ineffective against long, complex, and random passwords.
- **Time-Consuming:** Testing all possible combinations can take a lot of time, depending on the password's length and complexity.
- **Limited by Dictionary:** Dictionary attacks do not work if the password is not in the dictionary.

In conclusion, the dictionary attack is a relatively simple and effective hacking technique for weak passwords; however, longer and more complex passwords are not easily breakable by this method.

Chapter 2:
Dictionary Attack

The Dictionary Attack

A dictionary attack can be used in various contexts where guessing a password is necessary. Here are some examples:

- **User Accounts:** Dictionary attacks can be used to guess passwords for user accounts such as email accounts, social media, etc.
- **Servers:** Dictionary attacks can be used to guess passwords for servers such as web servers, database servers, FTP servers, etc.
- **Embedded Systems:** Dictionary attacks can be used to guess passwords for embedded systems such as surveillance cameras, routers, network printers, etc.
- **Mobile Applications:** Dictionary attacks can be used to guess passwords for mobile applications such as messaging apps, online games, etc.

Note that dictionary attacks are often used in conjunction with other techniques.

Here are some scenarios where dictionary attacks can be used in combination with other techniques:

- **Social Engineering:** Attackers can use social engineering techniques to obtain information about the victim, such as their name, birthdate, interests, etc.
- **Code Injection:** Attackers can use code injection techniques to bypass security measures in place to protect passwords.
- **Phishing Attacks:** Attackers can use phishing techniques to trick victims into disclosing their passwords. For example, they can create fake login pages that resemble those of popular online services such as Gmail or Facebook and ask the victim to enter their username and password. Attackers can then use this information to launch a dictionary attack against other accounts of the victim.

Chapter 2:
Dictionary Attack

Historical Hacks Caused by Weak Passwords:

- **Yahoo Hack in 2013:** Hackers gained access to over 3 billion Yahoo accounts using an easy-to-guess password: "password."

- **LinkedIn Hack in 2012:** More than 167 million LinkedIn accounts were compromised due to a weak password: "linkedin."

- **Sony Pictures Hack in 2014:** Hackers used weak and reused passwords to access Sony Pictures' network, allowing them to steal confidential information.

- **Target Hack in 2013:** Hackers managed to steal information from 40 million Target customers by using a weak password obtained from a third-party vendor.

- **Mat Honan Hack in 2012:** Hackers accessed Mat Honan's accounts, a Wired journalist, using a weak password and exploiting security flaws in Apple and Google cloud storage accounts.

Chapter 2:
Dictionary Attack

The Basics of Dictionary Attacks

For attacking a Wi-Fi access point using a dictionary attack, we will primarily use the aircrack-ng suite and cupp3, a personalized password generator.

To launch the attack, we will follow these steps:

- **Correctly Identify the Target:** Collect necessary information about the target network, such as its SSID, BSSID, channels used, and connected clients.

- **Monitor the Target Access Point:** Use the airodump-ng tool to capture the data packets circulating on the network, focusing only on the target access point.

- **Perform Deauthentication**: Disconnect clients connected to the access point to capture the handshake, a control message exchanged between the access point and the client during the connection establishment.

- **Create a Password Dictionary:** Use the cupp3 tool to generate passwords based on information such as the target's name, user name, etc.

- **Launch the Attack:** Use aircrack-ng to test each password in the dictionary against the captured handshake until the correct security key is found.

It is essential to understand that each Wi-Fi access point can have different configurations in terms of channel, power, encryption, and security.

Therefore, it is important to take the time to gather information about the target network before launching a dictionary attack.

Additionally, some networks may have implemented additional security measures to counter such attacks, such as MAC address filtering. It is crucial to adapt to each situation by using appropriate tools and techniques to bypass these additional security measures.

Chapter 2:
Dictionary Attack

Discovering Wireless Networks

After switching my network card to monitor mode (using airmon-ng or the ip command), I used the airodump-ng tool to scan the wireless networks within range of my device. This tool allowed me to gather information about the available networks, such as network names (SSID), MAC addresses of access points (BSSID), and the channels in use.

Next, I used the --bssid and -c options to focus on the specific access point I had set up for the occasion. The --bssid option allowed me to specify the MAC address of the access point, while the -c option allowed me to specify the channel used by the access point. Additionally, I used the -w option with airodump-ng to save the capture to a file.

The command I used was:

- airodump-ng [monitor interface] --bssid [AP MAC address] -c 6 -w databook

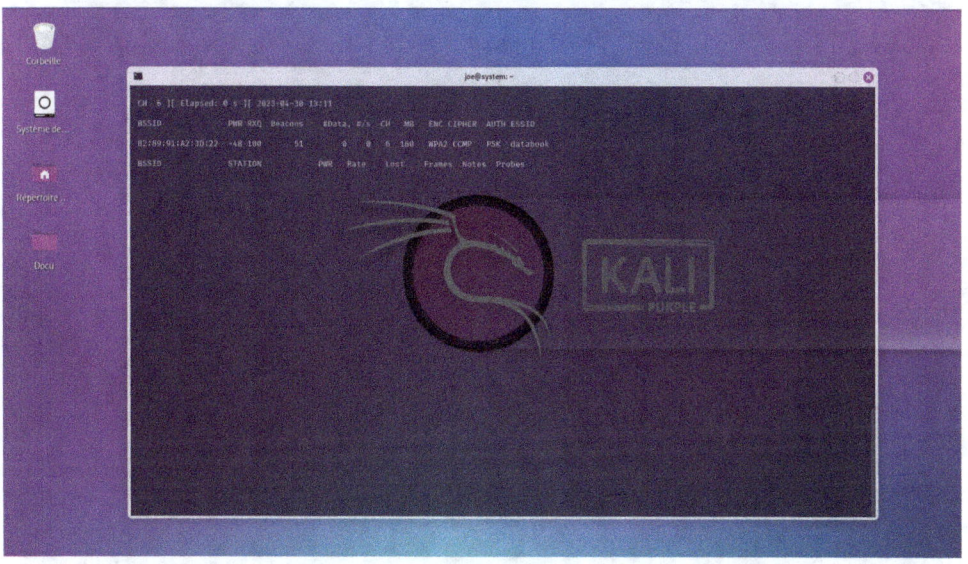

The option -w allowed me to specify the capture file name where all collected information would be saved, including the famous handshake.

This step is crucial as it enables the preservation of all data collected during the wireless network scanning process.

It's important to note that using these tools to test the security of wireless networks without prior authorization from the network owner is illegal. Therefore, it's crucial to respect privacy and the rights of others when using these tools. However, detecting wireless networks within range of your device is a critical step in safeguarding both home and professional networks. It allows for checking the security of one's own network and taking measures to prevent potential attacks by malicious hackers.

Chapter 2:
Dictionary Attack

Capturing the Handshake

The next step involves de-authenticating clients connected to the network. This allows us to force clients to temporarily disconnect and initiate the handshake exchange when they reconnect.

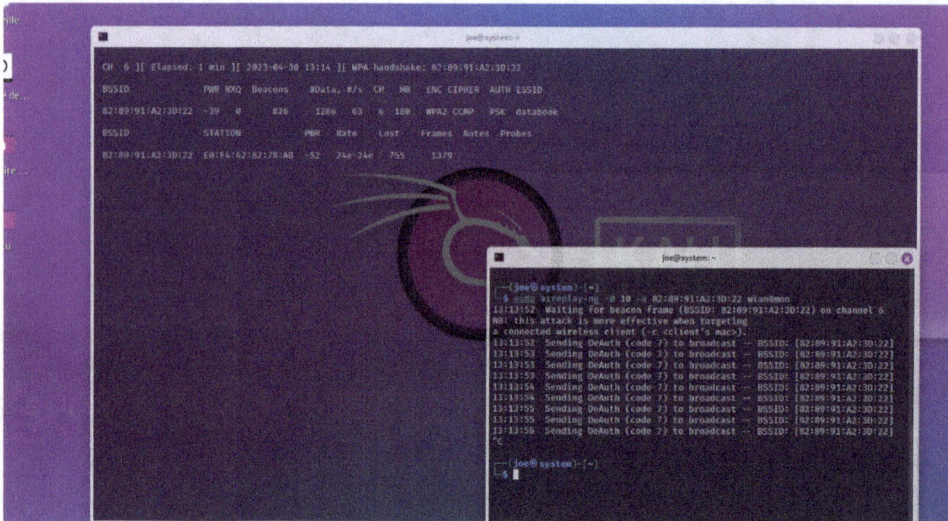

Once we have captured the handshake, we can stop the attack and use aircrack-ng to launch a dictionary attack. We can either use a list of common passwords or create our own list using a tool like Cupp3.

It's important to emphasize that this dictionary attack is based on the assumption that the password is weak.

For this example, I used Cupp3.

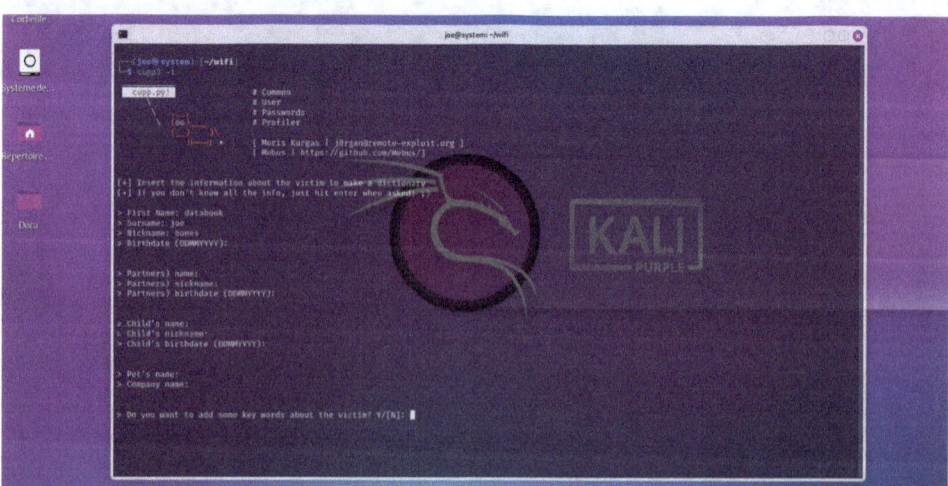

Chapter 2:
Dictionary Attack

WPA Cracking

Once we have captured the handshake of the target network using airodump-ng, we need a way to decrypt it. This is where the dictionary comes into play. The dictionary is a list of passwords that will be used by aircrack-ng to attempt to decrypt the handshake.

Using our dictionary, aircrack-ng will try each password in the list to crack the handshake. If the correct password is found in the dictionary, aircrack-ng will stop the attack and return the password!

If our dictionary does not contain the correct password, we will not be able to decrypt the handshake. That's why it's recommended to create a custom dictionary using information about the target, such as names (like the AP name if customized), birthdays, commonly used words, etc.

Once we have captured the handshake of the target network and have our custom dictionary ready, we are ready to launch aircrack-ng to attempt to decrypt the handshake and retrieve the network's security key.

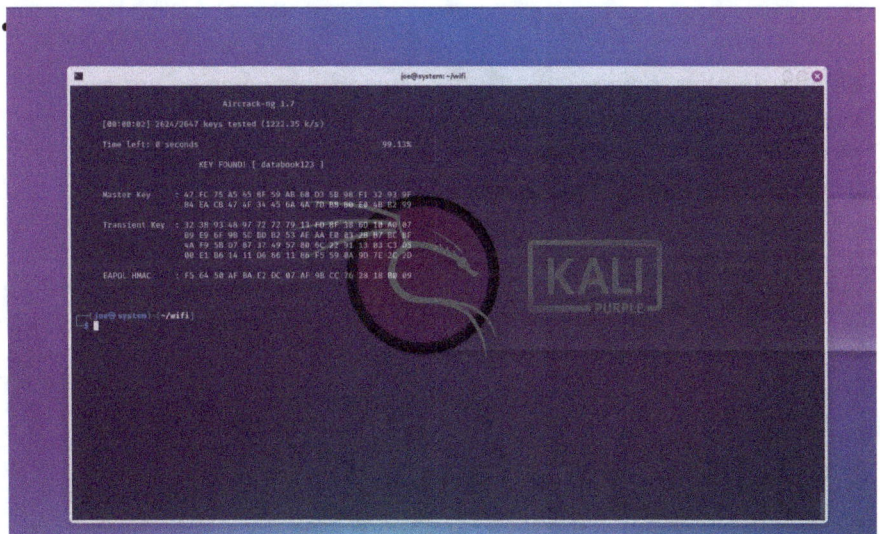

If the dictionary attack does not yield satisfactory results, we will use a "rogue AP" attack instead. This involves creating a "trap" access point that impersonates the target network and encourages users to connect to it. This attack is often more complex to execute but can be very effective for gaining access to the network if the dictionary attack fails.

Chapter 2:
Dictionary Attack

Creating an Effective Dictionary

To create a good password dictionary, it is recommended to combine several techniques to maximize the success chances of the dictionary attack.

One common technique is to use tools like CUPP3 and Crunch to generate custom passwords based on information you have about the target. This can include names (such as the AP name or others), birthdays, commonly used words, etc.

In addition to this, you can also include lists of common passwords or dictionaries provided with certain tools in your dictionary to increase the success rate of the attack.

It's important to keep in mind that the larger your dictionary, the longer it will take to try each password. A dictionary that is too large can slow down the cracking process and may not be effective due to the time required to go through it. Therefore, finding a balance between the size of your dictionary and the likelihood of including the correct password is crucial.

By combining techniques like CUPP3, Crunch, and common password lists, you can create a "super dictionary" to maximize the success of the dictionary attack. Remember that your dictionary size should be sufficient to be effective but not so large that it slows down the cracking process.

Chapter 2:
Dictionary Attack

Creating an Effective Dictionary

The dictionary attack is one of the most common methods for cracking a WPA/WPA2 password. In this method, the attacker uses a predefined list of passwords to try to guess the password of a wireless network. Therefore, the quality and relevance of the password list are key elements for the success of the attack.

Here's how to create an effective dictionary:

- **Retrieve a list of common passwords and/or common patterns.**
  Some are available in the Kali repository or already installed in /usr/share/.

- **Create your own list of potential passwords using the Cupp3** tool in interactive mode (-i). Cupp3 allows you to create a customized password list based on information you have about the victim, such as their name, date of birth, or familiar keywords.

- **You can also request an artificial intelligence like ChatGPT** to generate passwords with iterations from a given string. ChatGPT is an AI trained to understand and generate text based on input provided. You can give it a keyword or phrase, and it will generate a list of passwords using different iterations.

- **Finally, to create your final password list**, merge all your password files and use Linux commands to remove duplicates and passwords with less than eight characters. You can use "cat" to merge files, "sort -u" to remove duplicates, and "grep -vE '^.{0,7}$'" to remove passwords with less than eight characters.

Once you have created your initial dictionary using the tips mentioned above, you can pass it through the Cupp3 tool again with the -w option to generate even more iterations and combinations. This can be very useful to increase the success chances of the dictionary attack.

However, note that this will significantly increase the size of the dictionary, which may impact the performance of the attack. Therefore, it is advisable to limit the size of the dictionary and focus on the most likely passwords rather than trying to generate all possible combinations.

Chapter 2:
Dictionary Attack

Defense / Protection

Here are some additional recommended practices to protect your Wi-Fi network against dictionary-type attacks:

- **Use a strong password:** Using a strong password is essential to protect your Wi-Fi network against brute-force attacks. A strong password typically consists of a combination of uppercase letters, lowercase letters, numbers, and special characters. It is recommended to use a password of at least 12 characters long, but the longer and more complex the password, the harder it is for attackers to guess.

- **It's also important never to reuse the same password for different accounts,** APs, devices, or others, because if one password is compromised, all accounts/APs/ etc. using the same password may be compromised.

- **Change your password regularly to avoid long-term compromises.**

- **Disable WPS: Disabling Wi-Fi Protected Setup (WPS) is a recommended** security measure because this feature can be vulnerable to attacks. Some WPS protocols are vulnerable to attacks, such as the brute-force PIN attack method, which can allow an attacker to access the Wi-Fi network by guessing the WPS PIN code. Therefore, it is advised to disable WPS in the Wi-Fi router settings.

- **Use MAC filtering:** You can configure your router to only accept connections from approved MAC addresses. This will prevent attackers from accessing your Wi-Fi network even if they know the password, and can be effective in restricting access to your Wi-Fi network, but it also has limitations. Firstly, maintaining a list of approved MAC addresses can be cumbersome, especially in a home network where devices are frequently added or replaced. Moreover, it is relatively easy for a skilled attacker to spoof a MAC address and impersonate an approved device.

- **Update firmware:** Make sure to keep your router firmware up to date to fix known vulnerabilities.

- **Not broadcasting the SSID can make the Wi-Fi network less visible to unauthorized users,** but it can also make network usage less convenient in some cases because users must manually enter the network name to connect. Additionally, disabling SSID broadcasting will not prevent a determined attacker from identifying and targeting the network. Therefore, this depends on how you use your AP.

Chapter 3:
Rogue AP Attacks (Advanced)

Introduction to the Attack

Rogue AP attacks are considered one of the most sophisticated methods for hacking wireless networks.

A rogue AP attack involves creating a fake access point to deceive users into connecting to a malicious network. This technique is often used for espionage, data theft, or phishing.

To conduct a rogue AP attack, a specific tool is required to launch the attack quickly.

In this book, we will use a tool I developed specifically for this purpose. The tool utilizes Hostapd among other components to create a fake access point.

Here's a summarized overview of how it works:

- We will use the SSID and BSSID retrieved during the initial attack.

- The tool uses Hostapd to create an AP identical to the chosen access point.

- Iptables rules, a DHCP server, DNS spoofing, and a web server are set up.

- The tool initiates a de-authentication attack in a loop to force clients to reconnect.

- Clients then reconnect to the Rogue AP created by the tool and are redirected to the web server.

- On this page, a request for the WPA password is made, intentionally designed to look basic (but it could resemble an official router or captive portal authentication page).

- Finally, the tool verifies the password's validity using aircrack-ng.

This method underscores the importance of caution when connecting to Wi-Fi networks and verifying the authenticity of the authentication page.

Chapter 3:
Rogue AP Attacks (Advanced)

Introduction to the Attack

Rogue AP attacks are sophisticated methods used by hackers to gain unauthorized access to wireless networks and steal sensitive data.

In this chapter, I will show you how these attacks work and how you can protect yourself against them.

If dictionary attacks fail, hackers may resort to a more sophisticated method called Rogue AP.

When a user connects to a Wi-Fi network for the first time, they may configure their device to automatically connect to that network whenever it's available.

Hackers can exploit this feature by creating a malicious access point with the same name as the legitimate Wi-Fi network and emitting disruptive signals to jam the original AP's signal. When the user's device detects the malicious access point, it may automatically connect to it without the user realizing the deception.

Once the fake access point is created, a DHCP server and a web server with a fake page are set up. DNS Spoofing can be used to redirect clients to the fraudulent web server, or a script verifies in real-time if the password entered by the user matches that of the target AP (using the handshake).

The setup process can sometimes be lengthy and tedious. That's why I have developed a tool that greatly simplifies this task by automating all necessary steps, allowing for a much faster transition from setup to execution.

Custom tool development is an excellent way for developers to deepen their knowledge and mastery of the programming languages they use. It also helps them better understand tool functionality, which can aid in quicker and more effective issue resolution when using it.

A custom tool is designed to meet specific user needs and offers unique features that may not be available in standard tools.

Chapter 3:
Rogue AP Attacks (Advanced)

Strengths:

- This attack can be highly effective because it exploits users' trust in wireless networks. Users tend to automatically connect to a previously used wireless network without suspicion, making the attack easier to execute.

- The complexity of the password has no impact on the attack.

- Once a user connects to a malicious access point, hackers can potentially access all data flowing through the network, including usernames, passwords, credit card information, and other sensitive data.

- The flexibility arises from users being on the same local network as the attackers. This provides a wide range of opportunities for attackers to adapt their approach based on the target and the objectives of the attack.

Weaknesses:

- Rogue AP attacks require hackers to be physically close to the victim.

- The attack can be detected if users are vigilant.

- For this attack to succeed, users must have configured their device to automatically connect to a wireless network, which can be avoided by disabling this feature or removing unnecessary Wi-Fi networks from their list of saved networks.

- Depends on user gullibility. If a user is cautious, the attack will be less effective.

- If users use VPN connections, it can make it more difficult for hackers to intercept sensitive data.

Chapter 3:
Rogue AP Attacks (Advanced)

There have been several hacking stories involving rogue access points (APs) over the years.

- **One of the most well-known stories is the attack against TJX in 2007.** TJX is a chain of stores that was hacked via a rogue AP. Hackers placed a fake WiFi access point in one of the chain's stores, which was used to steal credit card information from millions of customers.

- **Another famous hacking story involving a rogue AP is the attack at the Black Hat conference in 2008.** Hackers set up a fake WiFi access point named "Free Public WiFi," which attracted many conference attendees to connect. The hackers were able to intercept traffic and access sensitive user data.

- **In 2010, a man was convicted for setting up a rogue AP in a conference room in New York** during a meeting of the American Federation of Labor and Congress of Industrial Organizations (AFL-CIO). He used a modified WiFi antenna to create a fake access point connected to a laptop. Meeting participants were prompted to connect to the wireless network, allowing the hacker to capture their usernames and passwords. The hacker was eventually arrested and convicted of identity theft.

- **In 2012, hackers installed a rogue WiFi access point at San Francisco Airport** to steal travelers' data. They created an unsecured WiFi network called "attwifi," which closely resembled the official WiFi network name of the airport ("SFO WiFi"). Many travelers connected to the insecure network, enabling hackers to intercept traffic and steal personal and financial information.

- **In 2014, a South Korean telecommunications company was hacked via a rogue AP.** Hackers set up a fake WiFi access point near the company and managed to lure employees into connecting to their unsecured network. This allowed hackers to access the company's networks and steal sensitive data. The hackers were eventually arrested and convicted for their crime.

Chapter 3:
Rogue AP Attacks (Advanced)

My Tool: Honey-Kit (Specifically the WebCrack Module)

In this chapter, I will introduce rogue AP attacks and the tool I developed in Bash.

Specifically, we will explore how to hack a secure Wi-Fi network using WPA or WPA2 by deploying a malicious access point.

Upon launching the tool, it performs a quick setup and prompts for which interfaces to use, as well as the name you wish to give to the AP:

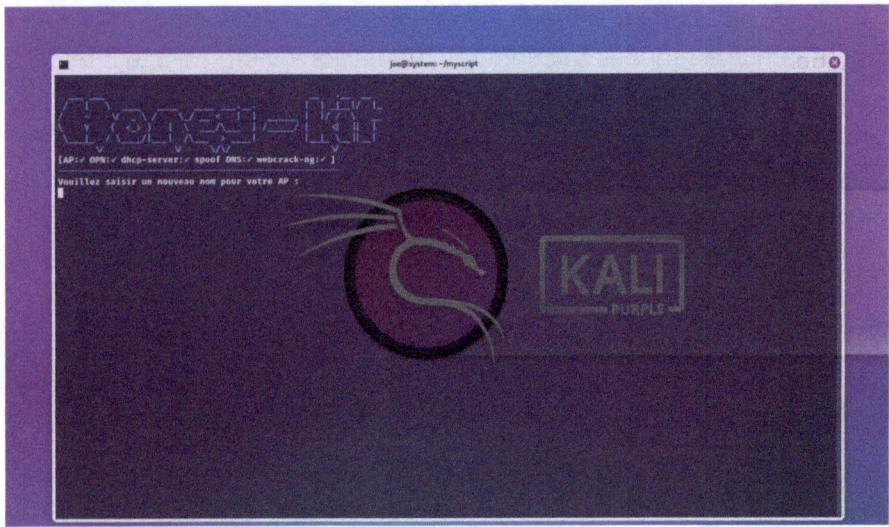

Then, the tool asks if you want to inject a Beef hook. This is JavaScript code generated by the "Beef-xss" tool, used for executing a Man-In-The-Browser (MITB) attack. (For now, we will answer "no" to this question, as we will cover this point in Chapter 5.)
Similarly, we will not activate the jammer for now.

At this stage, the operation is quite straightforward. Basic network configuration commands like **ifconfig** are used to configure the interfaces, and the **hostapd** configuration file is modified with the name entered by the user. This step essentially sets up the **malicious AP to function like a normal Wi-Fi access point,** capable of providing network connectivity to clients that connect to it.

Chapter 3:
Advanced Rogue AP Attacks

My Tool Honey-Kit (Specifically the WebCrack Module)

Next, the tool initiates the attack:

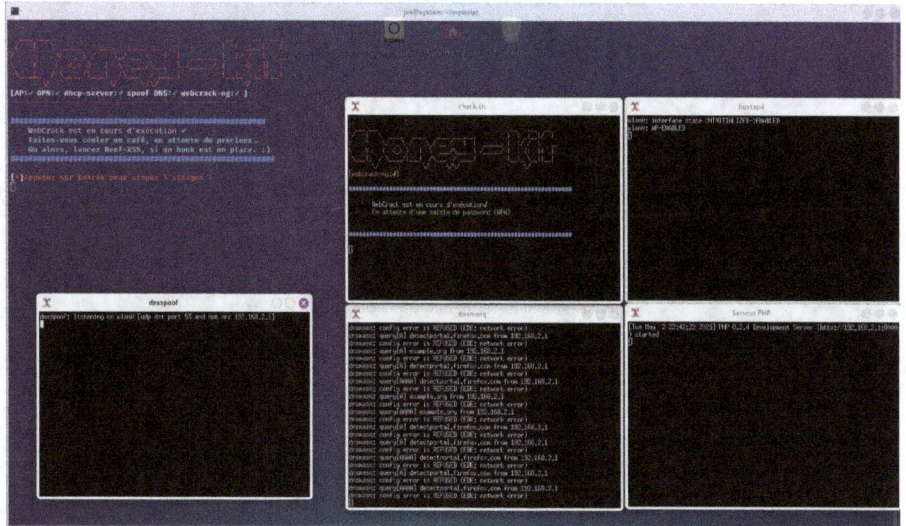

I'm not connected to the internet, which is why we're seeing errors in
the DNSMASQ logs.

Here we are, all necessary services have been set up. The tool has
deployed a functional access point using hostapd, a DHCP server using
dnsmasq to assign IP addresses to clients, DNS spoofing with dnsspoof,
and a web server with a script named "check" running to verify
passwords with the handshake. Each service is running in a separate
xterm window to allow precise control over each step of the process.

At the client side, the redirection is taking effect properly.

Chapter 3:
Rogue AP Attacks (Advanced)

My tool Honey-Kit (specifically the WebCrack module)

And when the client enters the correct WPA:

At this point, the client has reconnected to our access point (AP) and was redirected to our web server. They entered their WPA key, which was validated using Aircrack-ng on the handshake.

In this chapter, I presented my tool for conducting this rogue access point attack.

In summary,
the method involved cloning the target AP and deploying a DHCP server and a web server containing a phishing page to deceive users. Once users connected, we redirected them using DNS spoofing to access our fraudulent web server, where the script verified the password using the handshake.

However, it is important to emphasize that this method is illegal and can lead to serious legal consequences for those involved. Moreover, such attacks can cause significant harm to legitimate network users and may be considered a violation of their privacy and security.

Therefore, it is crucial to use this knowledge only for ethical and legal purposes, such as securing your own network. It is also important to educate users about the potential risks associated with using public or insecure Wi-Fi networks and to encourage them to take appropriate security measures to protect their sensitive information.

Automation vs. Manual Configuration of a Rogue AP Attack

In this guide, I've introduced my tool Honey-Kit, specifically the WebCrack module, designed to automate the complex process of a Rogue AP attack. This automation greatly simplifies deploying a malicious access point and testing WPA/WPA2 passwords using captured handshakes.

Why Use Honey-Kit?

Honey-Kit allows me to automate the deployment of a Rogue AP attack, providing several advantages:

- **Convenience and Efficiency:** Using Honey-Kit, I can quickly set up a malicious AP with a DHCP server, a web server containing a phishing page, and a password verification system using Aircrack-ng.

- **Reduced Error Management:** The tool handles technical details like configuring network interfaces, modifying configuration files (like hostapd), and launching necessary services (DHCP, DNS spoofing, web server).

- **Automation of Repetitive Tasks:** Honey-Kit automatically opens separate xterm windows for each service, making it easy to monitor and debug at each step of the process.

While Honey-Kit is designed to streamline the process, it is entirely possible to manually set up this attack. Here are the general steps involved:

- **Deploying the Access Point:** Use tools like hostapd to configure a malicious WiFi access point with the SSID and BSSID of the target AP.

- **Setting Up DHCP Server:** Configure a DHCP server using dnsmasq to assign IP addresses to clients connecting to the malicious AP.

- **DNS Spoofing:** Use dnsspoof to redirect client DNS traffic to a fraudulent DNS server, facilitating redirection to a phishing page.

- **Password Verification Script:** Write a custom script (e.g., Python or Bash) to automate password verification for each entry using the captured handshake with Aircrack-ng.

- **Phishing Web Page:** Create a web page containing a password entry form tailored to your attack, and set up a web server (such as Apache or Nginx) to host this page.

By following these manual steps, you can also successfully execute a Rogue AP attack, though it requires a deep understanding of networking technologies and more detailed management of configurations and services.

Chapter 3:
Advanced Rogue AP Attacks

My tool Honey-Kit (specifically the WebCrack module)

To execute this attack, hackers often use tools specifically designed for creating malicious access points. Using these tools provides several advantages, including:

- **Speed and Efficiency:** Rogue AP creation tools are designed to be fast and efficient, allowing hackers to set up the attack more quickly and successfully.

- **Customization**: Rogue AP creation tools enable hackers to customize attack parameters according to their specific needs, such as AP power, broadcast range, etc.

- **Automation:** Rogue AP creation tools can automate certain parts of the attack process, enabling hackers to focus on other aspects of the attack.

- **User-Friendliness:** Rogue AP creation tools are often designed to be user-friendly, making them accessible to hackers with varying skill levels.

Moreover, developing one's own tools for creating Rogue APs can offer several additional advantages. By developing their own tools, hackers can:

- **Further Customize Their Attack:** Hackers can tailor their tools to meet specific requirements, potentially increasing the effectiveness of their attack.

- **Gain a Competitive Edge:** By developing unique and powerful tools, hackers can gain a competitive advantage over others attempting similar attacks.

- **Enhance Hacking Skills:** Developing tools for creating Rogue APs can help hackers improve their hacking skills, making them more effective in other areas of cybersecurity.

The tool will be available on GitHub upon the book's release. However, the repository may initially be private. If you wish to access it, feel free to contact me via Twitter or Instagram, and I will provide access to the private repository.
https://github.com/pikabones

Chapter 4: MITB Attacks

The Basics of MITB Attacks

The Man in the Browser (MITB) attack is a sophisticated type of cyber attack that targets users' web browsers to steal confidential information.

This technique is becoming increasingly widespread and poses a significant threat to businesses and individuals conducting online transactions.
In this chapter, we will explore in detail how MITB attacks work, the different attack vectors, and the prevention methods to protect against this ever-evolving threat.

In the previous chapter, we attacked a Wi-Fi access point by copying its name. For you, I have imagined a small variant inspired by a story that happened to me with a friend.

The scenario is simple:

"I have already connected to an access point named "databook".

If I perform a Wi-Fi scan in monitor mode, I can see that my phone and computer are emitting "probes". **Probes are broadcast messages sent periodically by Wi-Fi devices to search for access points."**

The idea here is to create a Wi-Fi access point with the same name as "databook" and wait for my devices to connect to it automatically, thinking it is the legitimate access point they have previously encountered.

It is important to note that a classic Man In The Middle (MITM) attack typically occurs when we are connected to the same local network as our target.

In a traditional MITM attack, an attacker might use techniques such as ARP poisoning to intercept and manipulate communication between the target and the network gateway. This allows the attacker to eavesdrop, alter, or inject malicious content into the data stream without the target's knowledge.

However, in this scenario, if our machine is the router, we are technically already in a situation equivalent to MITM. By positioning ourselves as the router, we can intercept all traffic between connected devices and the internet, providing a powerful vantage point for capturing and manipulating data.

This elevated position eliminates the need for additional MITM techniques like ARP poisoning, as all data flows through our controlled access point by default.

In this chapter, we will explore two very common hacking techniques: phishing and reverse shell.

Phishing is a technique that involves deceiving users into providing confidential information such as usernames and passwords.

A reverse shell is a technique that allows a hacker to take control of a remote system. We will use Metasploit-Framework and a reverse shell.

Chapter 4:
Man In The Browser Attacks

Introduction to Beef-xss

Beef-xss, also known as **The Browser Exploitation Framework Project**, is an open-source penetration testing tool used to exploit web browsers. Developed using JavaScript, it offers significant flexibility for security testers when exploiting users' browsers.

One of the strengths of Beef-xss is that it allows security testers to send malicious links to users. When a user clicks on this link, they are redirected to a web page controlled by the attacker. This page contains malicious code that can be used to take control of the user's browser.

Beef-xss also offers features such as recording browser sessions and stealing cookies, which can be used to access users' online accounts. Additionally, the tool can be used to target specific users with phishing attacks by creating fake login pages.

However, a potential weakness of Beef-xss is that the tool can be detected by certain security systems. Antivirus software may detect the malicious code, and firewalls may block access to the attacker-controlled page. Therefore, it is important for security testers to be aware of these limitations when using the tool.

In the context of this chapter, we will deliberately use a classic Beef injection and standard payloads that might be detected by antivirus software. However, it is important to note that evading antivirus software is a vast and complex subject that requires advanced knowledge in computer security. We will not cover this topic in this book, but we encourage readers to further their knowledge on this subject if necessary.

Chapter 4:
Man In The Browser Attacks

Introduction to Beef-xss

The user interface of Beef-xss is accessible via a web interface, which greatly simplifies its use. The user can navigate through the different menus to configure the tool's settings and generate injectable JavaScript scripts. These scripts can be injected into a web page and used to target the browsers of users who access this page.

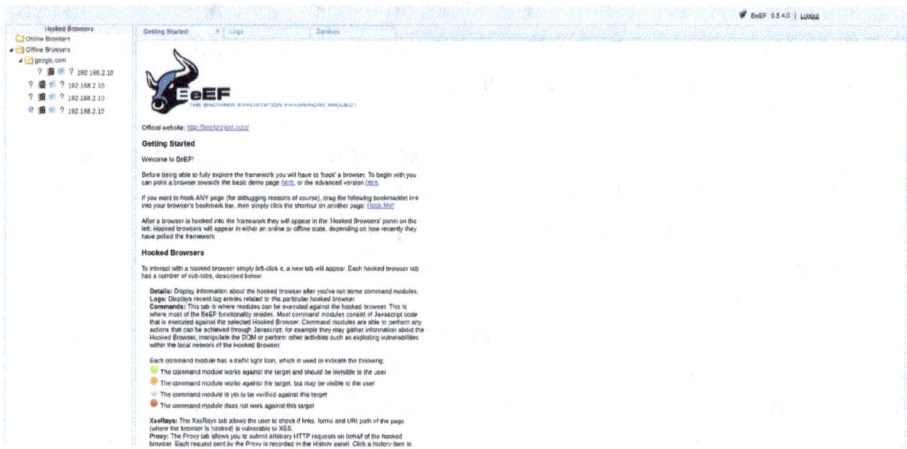

Once the script is injected, the user's browser is compromised and controlled remotely by the attacker via the Beef-xss web interface. This allows the attacker to launch phishing attacks, cookie theft, and other types of attacks against the user.

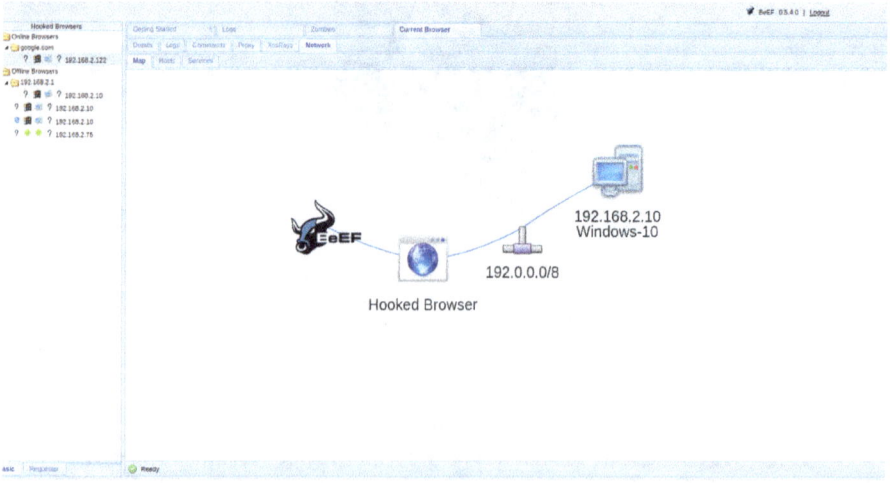

Chapter 4:
Man In The Browser Attacks

The MITB Attack

After restarting my custom tool, I activated the "Beef hook" for all the pages on our server. This means that every client who opens their browser and visits a page hosted on our server is susceptible to being attacked with various malicious payloads.

The malicious JavaScript code is injected into the web pages that load in the victim's browser. This code is executed client-side, meaning on the victim's browser, allowing attackers to intercept the data transmitted between the browser and the web server.

Beef-xss also offers a range of customization options for MITB attacks, such as adding phishing forms, redirecting the victim to a malicious site, or capturing screenshots of the victim's browser.

Here, for example, is a module to open a chat prompt.

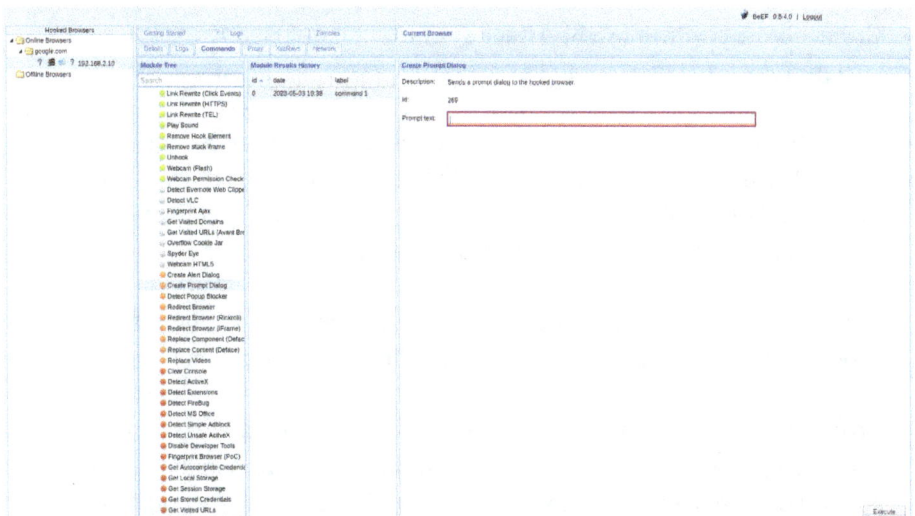

Note that I am using my tool (a rogue AP), but a JavaScript injection can be carried out in several ways.

During a MITM attack, the malicious script can be injected directly into web pages through techniques such as ARP spoofing or DNS spoofing.

It is also possible to exploit an XSS vulnerability on a website to inject malicious code into the pages viewed by users. Other attack vectors include captive portals, which are often used to provide public Wi-Fi access in places like airports and cafes.

Chapter 4:
Man In The Browser Attacks

Here are some of the common possibilities and attack vectors that BeEF can utilize:

- **Phishing:** BeEF can be used to create phishing pages and distribute them to users via emails, instant messages, or malicious links. Once users visit the phishing page, BeEF can be used to hack their browser and take control of their computer.

- **Script Injection**: BeEF can be used to inject malicious JavaScript code into web pages visited by users. This code can be used to redirect the user to malicious sites, steal login information, or perform other malicious actions.

- **Session Hijacking**: BeEF can be used to steal session cookies and take control of user accounts.

- **Denial of Service (DoS) Attacks:** BeEF can be used to launch denial of service attacks against websites, servers, or networks.

- **Cross-Site Scripting (XSS) Attacks:** BeEF can be used to exploit XSS vulnerabilities and take control of users' browsers.

- **Security Testing:** BeEF can be used to test web browser security vulnerabilities, such as CSRF vulnerabilities and browser library security flaws. BeEF is a legal tool intended for penetration testing and security purposes only. It should not be used for illegal or malicious activities.

- **Keylogger:** BeEF can be used to record users' keystrokes, thus retrieving information such as passwords, credit card numbers, and other sensitive data.

- **Brute Force Attacks**: BeEF can be used to launch brute force attacks against web login pages, user accounts, or password encryption systems. This method can be used to obtain credentials and access user accounts or protected systems. However, this method is generally less effective than other attack methods as it often requires a lot of time and resources to succeed.

- **Reverse Shell**: BeEF can also be used to send a malicious payload through social engineering techniques, such as creating fake Adobe Flash or Java updates. Users can be tricked into installing these updates by clicking on malicious links or visiting infected web pages.

Chapter 4:
Man In The Browser Attacks

Phishing

One of the default modules included in BeEF is the phishing test module. This module allows testers to check if users can be easily tricked into disclosing their credentials or other sensitive information by clicking on a malicious link or responding to a phishing email.

Gmail phishing module:

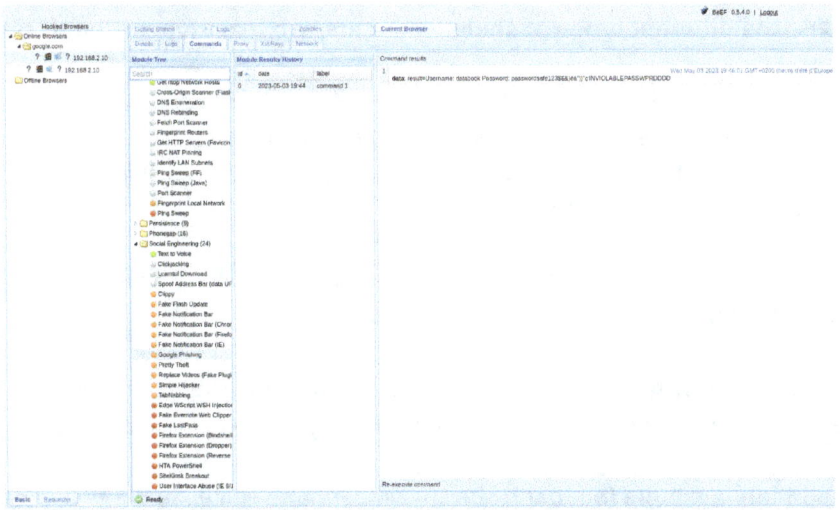

From the attacker's perspective:

The BeEF phishing test module can be used to create customized phishing pages that mimic the login pages of popular online services, such as Gmail or Facebook, and distribute them to victims. The credentials entered by victims on these phishing pages are then transmitted to BeEF, enabling testers to assess the effectiveness of user security measures and identify potential security vulnerabilities.

Chapter 4:
Man In The Browser Attacks

Reverse Shell

During pentesting, I often use a Meterpreter payload. One of the advantages of this payload is the variety of available modules that allow for a wide range of actions.

There are also other types of reverse shells that can be used depending on specific needs. Here are four other programs that can be used:

- **Netcat**: This is a networking utility that can create either a "bind" or "reverse" shell.

- **PHP:** PHP is a widely used scripting language for web development. It can be used to create a reverse shell by downloading a PHP script onto the target system. This script then connects to a remote server controlled by the attacker.

- **/bin/bash**: This shell is commonly used on Unix and Linux systems. It can create a reverse shell using the "nc" command to establish a connection back to the attacker.

- **Python**: Python is a popular programming language that can also be used to create a reverse shell. Python reverse shells can be created on both Windows and Linux systems, providing great flexibility.

Regarding the different types of shells, there are two main types: "bind" and "reverse".

"Bind" shells are created on the target system and wait for an attacker to connect. "**Reverse**" shells, on the other hand, are created on the attacker's side and connect back to the target system.

There are also different levels of sophistication, which vary based on available features and options.

For example, Meterpreter from Metasploit offers many advanced features such as screen capture, file theft, and VOIP call monitoring.

In comparison, a simple /bin/bash shell may offer more limited features but can be easier to implement and more discreet.

Depending on your needs, it is important to choose the type of reverse shell that best suits your situation.

Chapter 4:
Man In The Browser Attacks

Reverse Shell

When an attacker seeks to execute commands remotely on a web server, they can use a PHP reverse shell. However, this method is limited to the web server's directory structure, and the attacker can only access files accessible to the user under which the web server runs.

- **A classic reverse shell** executed by the user offers more freedom to access files and directories because the attacker connects as a user with elevated privileges.

- **Meterpreter reverse shells** offer more advanced features for post-exploitation attacks, such as webcam capture and audio recording.

- **Python Meterpreter** has a limited set of modules but is capable of performing advanced actions.

- **In contrast, Meterpreter Windows x64** has access to a wide variety of modules, allowing it to perform a broader range of actions such as password theft and screen capture, and can bypass firewalls and intrusion detection systems.

The choice will depend on the specific situation and the attacker's needs.

Why Bind or Reverse?

- **A bind shell** is a type of remote shell that listens on a specific port of a server and waits for a connection to be established with a remote client. When the attacker connects to this port, the bind shell grants remote access. For this method to work, the server must be accessible on the Internet, and the attacker needs to know the server's public IP address and the port number used by the bind shell. This can be problematic if the server is behind a firewall or NAT router that masks its public IP address and assigns a private IP address. In such cases, it is difficult for the attacker to connect to the server using a bind shell.

- **On the other hand, a reverse shell** is a type of remote shell that connects back to a remote attacker, typically using an arbitrary port on the attacker's computer. This allows the attacker to connect to a remote server without needing to know the server's public IP address. In this case, the server sends an outgoing connection request to the attacker, who is outside the firewall or NAT router. Thus, the firewall or NAT router does not block the outgoing connection because it was initiated by the server, enabling the attacker to connect to the remote server. This method can bypass restrictions related to private IP addresses and firewalls.

Chapter 4:
Man In The Browser Attacks

Metasploit Framework

Metasploit Framework is an open-source penetration testing platform used for the development and execution of exploits and security vulnerabilities. It was created by H.D. Moore in 2003 and is now maintained by Rapid7.

The Metasploit Framework uses a command-line interface and is based on Ruby. It provides a wide range of tools for analyzing and exploiting vulnerabilities in operating systems, applications, and network protocols.

The modular system of the Metasploit Framework allows users to create and customize exploit modules, payloads, encoders, post-exploitation modules, and auxiliary tools.

Exploits are modules that leverage a vulnerability in a system or application to execute malicious code or gain remote control of the system. Payloads are codes that are injected into the target system after exploiting the vulnerability.

Encoders are used to evade detection by security systems by encoding payloads so that they are not recognized by antivirus software.

Auxiliary modules provide additional functionalities such as vulnerability discovery and information gathering.

Metasploit Framework also comes with features like session management, which allows users to interact with remote shell sessions, post-exploitation tools for lateral movement and privilege escalation, and report generation, providing detailed reports on penetration testing.

The Metasploit Framework is continuously updated to address new vulnerabilities and attack techniques. It is used by security professionals, penetration testers, network administrators, and ethical hackers to test the security of computer systems and to train individuals in defending against cyber attacks.

Chapitre 4 :
Les attaques Man In The Browser

Metasploit Framework

Meterpreter est un outil puissant de post-exploitation utilisé dans le cadre du hacking éthique. Il permet d'avoir un accès distant à un système cible après une intrusion réussie et d'interagir avec ce système de manière transparente et discrète.

Meterpreter est une charge utile (payload) de Metasploit Framework qui s'exécute sur le système cible une fois qu'il a été compromis. Il utilise une technique de "staging" pour charger une petite partie de la charge utile initiale sur le système cible, qui sert ensuite de point d'entrée pour le reste de la charge utile. Cela permet à Meterpreter de contourner les pare-feu et autres mécanismes de sécurité.

Il est conçu pour être modulaire, ce qui signifie qu'il peut être étendu avec des plugins pour ajouter de nouvelles fonctionnalités. Il est également écrit en Ruby, un langage de programmation facile à lire et à écrire, ce qui facilite la création de nouveaux plugins.

Il est également capable de contourner les mécanismes de sécurité tels que l'authentification, le chiffrement et les pare-feu. Il peut utiliser des techniques d'encodage pour masquer son trafic et éviter la détection par les systèmes de sécurité.

Voici dix modules parmis les plus connus de Meterpreter :

Port scanner : ce module permet de scanner les ports ouverts sur un système cible pour identifier les services qui y sont associés.

- Keylogger : un module qui permet d'enregistrer les frappes de clavier effectuées sur le système cible.
- Screenshot : un module qui permet de prendre des captures d'écran du bureau de l'utilisateur sur le système cible.
- Persistence : un module qui permet d'installer un backdoor persistant sur le système cible pour une exploitation à long terme.
- Webcam snap : un module qui permet de prendre des photos à partir de la webcam du système cible.
- File system : un module qui permet d'accéder et de manipuler les fichiers sur le système cible.
- Privilege escalation : un module qui permet de trouver et d'exploiter des vulnérabilités pour élever les privilèges de l'utilisateur actuel.
- Password dumper : un module qui permet de récupérer les mots de passe stockés sur le système cible.
- Network sniffer : un module qui permet de capturer et d'analyser le trafic réseau sur le système cible.
- DLL injection : un module qui permet d'injecter du code malveillant dans les bibliothèques partagées d'un processus en cours d'exécution.

Chapter 4:
Man In The Browser Attacks

Metasploit Framework

Meterpreter is one of the most popular payloads in Metasploit, allowing attackers to access an interactive shell on a target machine, providing them with complete control over the system.

Here is a list of different types of Meterpreter payloads available in Metasploit:

- **Meterpreter Reverse TCP:** This payload is used to establish a connection from the target machine to the attacker's system using the TCP protocol. It enables attackers to remotely control the target system.

- **Meterpreter Reverse HTTPS**: This payload is similar to Meterpreter Reverse TCP but uses the HTTPS protocol to communicate with the attacker's system. It is more difficult to detect and block than the Reverse TCP payload.

- **Meterpreter Reverse HTTP:** This payload is similar to Meterpreter Reverse HTTPS but uses the HTTP protocol to communicate with the attacker's system. It is less secure than Reverse HTTPS but useful in environments where HTTPS is blocked.

- **Meterpreter Reverse DNS:** This payload is used to establish a connection from the target machine to the attacker's system using the DNS protocol. It is often used to bypass firewalls that block TCP and HTTP connections.

- **Meterpreter Reverse ICMP:** This payload is used to establish a connection from the target machine to the attacker's system using the ICMP protocol. It is often used to bypass firewalls that block TCP and HTTP connections.

- **Meterpreter Bind TCP:** This payload is used to listen on a specific port of the target machine and wait for an attacker's system to connect to this port. It is often used in attacks where the attacker cannot initiate the connection from their system.

- **Meterpreter Bind HTTPS:** This payload is similar to Meterpreter Bind TCP but uses the HTTPS protocol to communicate with the attacker's system. It is more difficult to detect and block than the Bind TCP payload.

The use of these payloads should be conducted for ethical and legal purposes, within the scope of authorized penetration testing and with explicit consent from the owners of the target systems

Chapter 4:
Man In The Browser Attacks

The module I've chosen allows me to deploy a payload disguised as a fake Adobe update, using a .bat file as the payload to evade detection by the browser.
(To create the payload, I used Metasploit, but there are many tools available in Kali.)

On the client side:

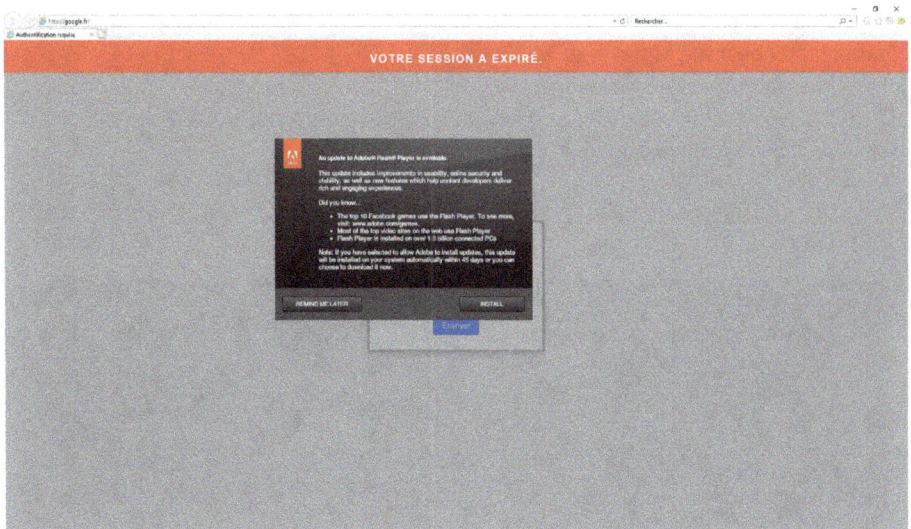

On the attacker side, I start the handler on Metasploit using the command "use exploit/multi/handler".

Chapter 4:
Man In The Browser Attacks

Once the payload is executed on the target machine, it establishes a connection with the listener configured on the Metasploit handler. The handler is then notified of the incoming connection and can establish a session with the target machine.

The handler acts as a central control point for the session established between the target machine and the attacker. This means the attacker can use the handler to remotely execute commands on the target machine, download files, collect information about the target machine, and so on.

Once the payload successfully executes on the target machine, Metasploit's handler is notified and establishes a session with the target machine.

The attacker can then use the handler to control the target machine remotely:

For example, here the "sysinfo" module allows me to obtain information about the remote system, such as the hostname, operating system, and kernel version.

Once you have successfully established a connection with a Meterpreter shell on a target, any commands you type into this shell are executed directly on the remote system. This gives you direct control over the system, allowing you to execute commands and access sensitive information on the target.

By using modules in the form of commands, you can access advanced functionalities to perform specific tasks. These modules are designed to assist you in executing more advanced actions and gathering valuable information about the target. Additionally, they can be customized and tailored to meet your specific needs.

Chapter 4:
Man In The Browser Attacks

Modules

Metasploit modules are scripts or programs that can perform a wide variety of tasks during penetration testing. They are designed to be used with the Metasploit framework, which provides a platform for developing, deploying, and executing these modules. They are written in Ruby, an object-oriented programming language, and organized into categories based on their purpose or functionality.

Once you have executed a payload, such as Meterpreter, on a target machine, you can use modules to perform specific tasks on that machine.

For example, you can use an exploitation module to exploit a vulnerability on the target machine and gain privileged access, or a post-exploitation module to explore the target machine's network and find other vulnerable machines.

Here are some of the most commonly used modules:

- **stdapi:** This is the standard module for basic system commands, such as file retrieval, file sending, reading configuration files, file deletion, etc.

- **priv:** This module provides high-privilege functionalities to allow users to authenticate as administrators or steal access tokens for other system processes.

- **migrate:** This feature allows you to migrate to a different process on the target system, which can be useful for avoiding detection or accessing additional privileges.

- **getsystem**: This module automates migration to a SYSTEM process on the target system, thus providing higher-level access.

- **portfwd:** This module enables port forwarding to allow external programs to communicate with internal services, bypassing firewalls or network restrictions.

- **screenshot:** This feature allows you to take screenshots of the target machine, which can be useful for monitoring user activity.

- **keylog_recorder:** This module records keystrokes on the target machine and sends them to the Meterpreter server.

Chapter 4:
Man In The Browser Attacks

Metasploit modules can be manually executed using the Metasploit console, or automated using scripts or third-party programs that connect to the Metasploit API.

Metasploit modules can also be customized or extended to meet the specific needs of a penetration test or attack. It is also possible to create custom modules from scratch using the Metasploit APIs.

Customizing existing modules or creating new modules can be useful in situations where existing modules do not meet the attacker's needs or are not discreet enough to avoid detection. This may also be necessary when the attacker targets a specific system that is not covered by existing module targets.

Adding functionality to existing modules can also be beneficial. For example, existing modules may not have the ability to perform certain actions, such as retrieving sensitive files or disabling antivirus security.

By adding these features, the attacker can increase the chances of success of their attack.

Note that customizing modules or creating new modules requires advanced knowledge of programming and computer security.

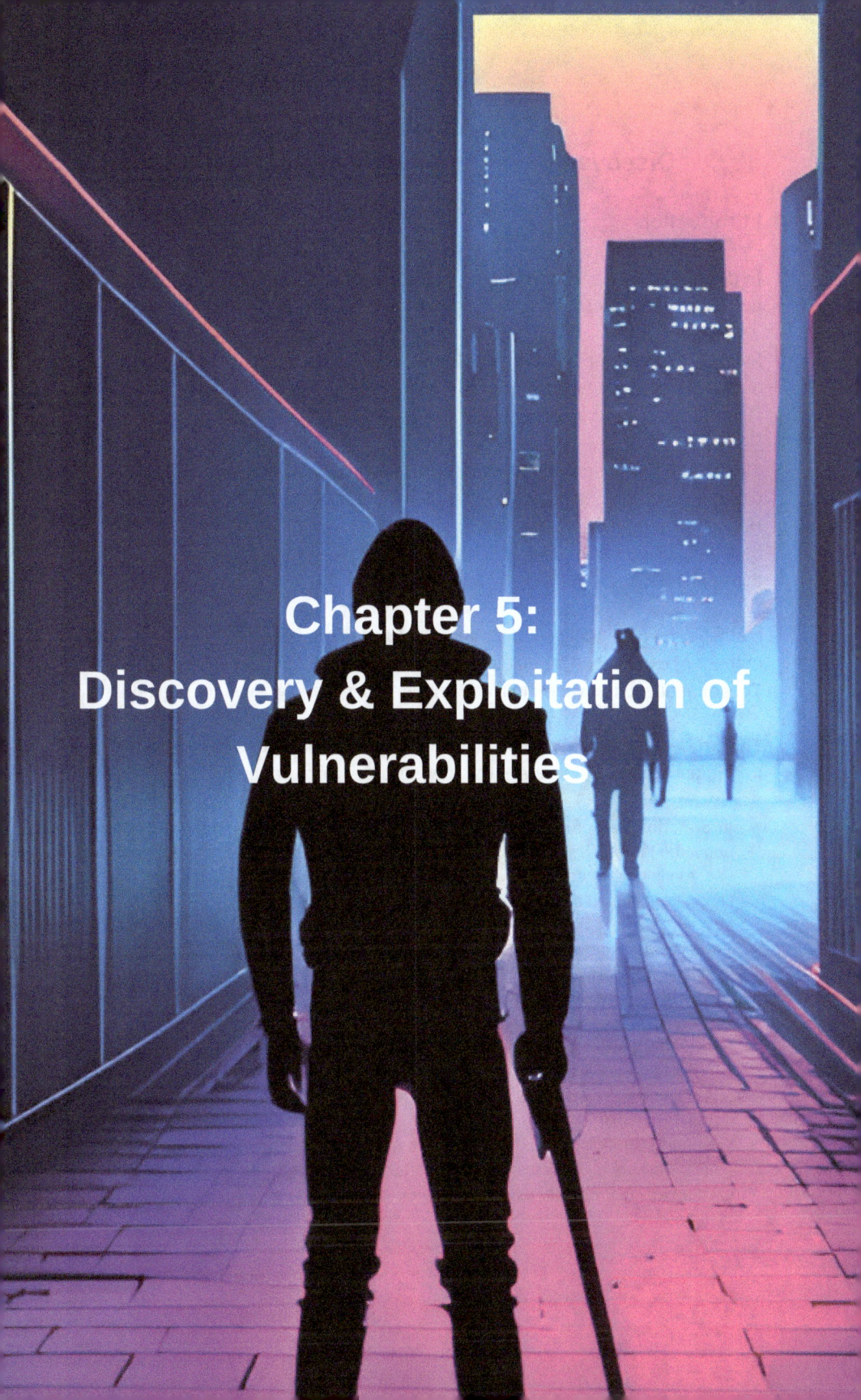

Chapter 5:
Discovery & Exploitation of
Vulnerabilities

Chapter 5:
Discovery and Exploitation of Vulnerabilities

Introduction

In this chapter, we will discuss the discovery and exploitation of vulnerabilities, a crucial topic for any hacker.

Firstly, it's important to note that vulnerabilities can be discovered in various ways. One of the most common methods is to scan networks and systems for known vulnerabilities using tools such as Nessus, OpenVAS, or Nmap.

These tools can identify common security flaws such as software vulnerabilities or open ports. Once a vulnerability is identified, the next step is exploitation. Hackers can employ various exploitation techniques, including injecting malicious code, exploiting security flaws in web applications, or leveraging vulnerabilities in third-party software like web browsers.

Metasploit is commonly used for vulnerability exploitation and contains a large number of exploitation modules that can be used for common vulnerabilities. These modules are written in Ruby and are user-friendly, even for beginners.

The process of discovering and exploiting vulnerabilities is a crucial step in hacker activities. Here are the key steps of this process:

- **Information Gathering:** The first step is to gather as much information as possible about the target. This may include details about the operating system, applications in use, running services, open ports, etc. Commonly used tools for this step include Nmap, Netcat, and manual reconnaissance.

- **Vulnerability Analysis:** Once sufficient information has been collected, the next step is to analyze potential vulnerabilities. Tools such as Nessus, OpenVAS, and Metasploit can be used to analyze known or potential vulnerabilities.

- **Formulating an Attack Plan:** The next step involves formulating an attack plan based on the information gathered in the previous steps. This plan may include tactics such as code injection, creating backdoors, privilege escalation, etc.

- **Executing the Attack:** The final step is to execute the attack using the plan formulated earlier. Hackers can use tools such as Metasploit, Cobalt Strike, and Empire to execute their attack plan.

It's important to emphasize that this entire process should be carried out with utmost caution and with prior permission from the owner of the targeted system, as part of a legal penetration test.

Chapter 5:
Discovery and Exploitation of Vulnerabilities

In this chapter, we will explore how to identify and exploit a vulnerability in software on a remote machine.

To do this, I have installed vulnerable software on a target machine.

We will begin by scanning our target using nmap to identify different services and their versions. Once this step is completed, we can search for known vulnerabilities associated with these services or software. To accomplish this, we will use the exploitdb database, which catalogs numerous known vulnerabilities and associated exploits.

There are numerous methods for exploiting software, services, or protocols. Among these, we can mention:

- Protocol hijacking such as ARP, DNS, IP, TCP, etc.
- Utilizing existing exploits for known vulnerabilities
- Creating your own tools or exploits for specific vulnerabilities
- Social engineering, which involves manipulating users to obtain sensitive information or access systems

In addition to these methods, there are also other techniques such as reverse engineering, code analysis, network traffic analysis, exploiting physical weaknesses, and many more.

In this chapter, we will focus on using existing exploits as a preliminary approach to familiarize ourselves with the subject.

An exploit is a program or technique that leverages a known vulnerability in software or a service to take control of the target machine. Exploits can be used for various tasks, such as recovering passwords, unauthorized access to data, remote command execution, etc.

While it is possible to create custom exploits for specific vulnerabilities, this may require advanced programming and cybersecurity skills. Moreover, developing an exploit can be time-consuming and challenging. Therefore, for this chapter, we will stick to using existing exploits.

Exploiting vulnerabilities can be illegal if done without authorization on systems belonging to third parties. It is crucial to always obtain permission from the system administrator or owner before proceeding with any vulnerability exploitation.

Chapter 5:
Discovery and Exploitation of Vulnerabilities

Tools

Detection and exploitation tools for vulnerabilities are essential for intermediate-level hackers as they enable them to discover weaknesses in target systems and exploit them to gain unauthorized access. These tools often use port and service analysis techniques to identify vulnerabilities and exploit them using preconfigured scripts or modules.

Here is a list of vulnerability detection and exploitation tools for an intermediate-level hacker:

- **Metasploit Framework:** A penetration testing tool that allows testing the security of systems and finding vulnerabilities.

- **Nessus:** A vulnerability scanner that detects security flaws in networks and systems.

- **OpenVAS:** A vulnerability scanning tool used to analyze networks for security vulnerabilities.

- **Nmap:** A port scanner that discovers open ports on a system and the services associated with them.

- **Nikto:** A vulnerability scanner that detects security flaws in web applications.

- **Burp Suite:** A suite of tools for web application security testing, including a proxy, scanner, and intrusion tester.

- **SQLMap**: An SQL injection tool that detects security flaws in web applications using a database.

- **Hydra:** A brute-force tool that tests passwords by attempting password combinations.

- **John The Ripper:** A password cracking tool that finds passwords using dictionary and brute-force techniques.

- **Aircrack-ng:** A password cracking tool for Wi-Fi networks that retrieves WEP and WPA encryption keys.

It is important to note that the use of these tools should be within legal and ethical boundaries, and any malicious use can have serious legal consequences.

Chapitre 5 :
Découverte et exploitation de vulnérabilités

Nmap plus en détails

Petite liste des différents modes de scan de Nmap et des options associées à chacun :

- **Scan de port (TCP SYN scan)** : L'option associée à ce mode de scan est "-sS". Ce mode de scan est utilisé pour identifier les ports ouverts sur un hôte.

- **Scan de port (TCP connect scan)** : L'option associée à ce mode de scan est "-sT". Ce mode de scan est similaire au scan TCP SYN, mais il utilise une connexion TCP complète pour vérifier si le port est ouvert ou fermé.

- **Scan de port (UDP scan)** : L'option associée à ce mode de scan est "-sU". Ce mode de scan est utilisé pour identifier les ports UDP ouverts sur un hôte.

- **Scan de script (NSE scan)** : L'option associée à ce mode de scan est "-sC" ou "--script=default". Ce mode de scan permet d'exécuter des scripts Nmap pour identifier les vulnérabilités potentielles des hôtes ou des services. Il existe de nombreux scripts disponibles pour effectuer des tâches spécifiques, tels que :

- **Scan de système d'exploitation (OS detection scan)** : L'option associée à ce mode de scan est "-O". Ce mode de scan est utilisé pour identifier le système d'exploitation en cours d'exécution sur un hôte en analysant les réponses des paquets envoyés à l'hôte.

- **Scan de version (version detection scan)** : L'option associée à ce mode de scan est "-sV". Ce mode de scan permet d'identifier les versions des services en cours d'exécution sur un hôte en analysant les réponses des paquets envoyés à l'hôte.

Il existe de nombreux scripts disponibles pour le mode de scan de script (NSE scan) de Nmap, certains des plus courants sont :

- **"http-vuln-*"** : pour identifier les vulnérabilités sur les serveurs web
- **"smb-vuln-*"** : pour identifier les vulnérabilités sur les partages de fichiers SMB
- **"mysql-vuln-*"** : pour identifier les vulnérabilités sur les serveurs de base de données MySQL
- **"ftp-*"** : pour identifier les vulnérabilités sur les serveurs FTP
- **"ssh-*"** : pour identifier les vulnérabilités sur les serveurs SSH

Comme toujours la recherche de vulnérabilités et l'exploitation de ces dernières doivent être effectuées de manière éthique et légale, de préférence dans le cadre d'un test de pénétration autorisé et supervisé par des professionnels de la sécurité informatique.

Chapter 5:
Discovery and Exploitation of Vulnerabilities

Vulnerability Research

One of the key features of Metasploit is its database, which can be used to store information about targets, vulnerabilities, and exploits.

By using Metasploit with Nmap, it's possible to gather information about targets and store it in the Metasploit database. To do this, you can use the db_nmap command in Metasploit, which executes an Nmap scan and saves the results into the database.

The db_nmap command can be used to perform Nmap scans on a single host or an entire network. It can also specify specific Nmap options, such as quiet mode or UDP port scanning.

When you run the **db_nmap** command, Metasploit analyzes the results of the Nmap scan and records them in the database. The collected information may include details about discovered hosts, running services, open ports, known vulnerabilities, and software versions used.

Once the information is stored in the database, you can use it to select potential targets for attacks, plan attack strategies, or provide vulnerability information to other members of the penetration testing team.

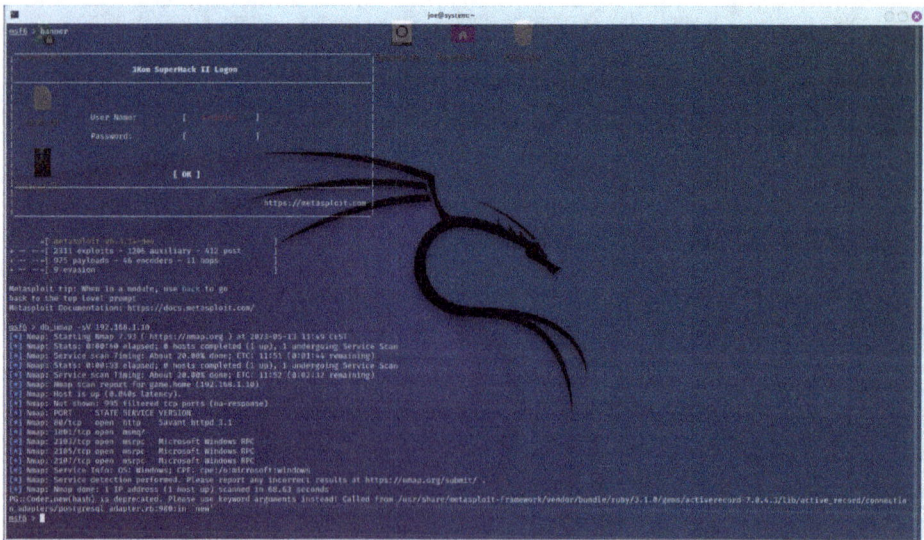

It appears that the web server is very old and obsolete, Savant 3.1. This web server is known to be vulnerable to many attacks and therefore represents a significant security risk to our system.

Chapter 5:
Discovery and Exploitation of Vulnerabilities

Vulnerability Discovery

It appears that the web server is vulnerable to an attack.

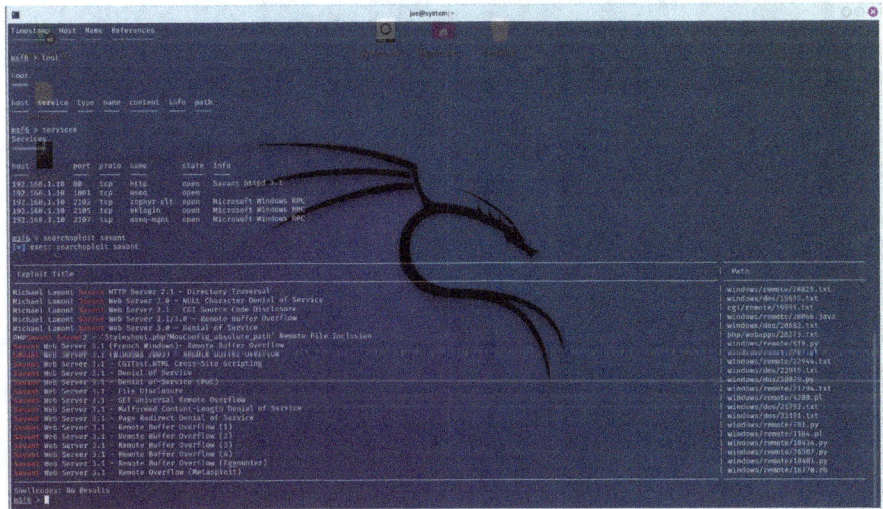

To check if there are known exploits that could be used to exploit this vulnerability, I use the 'searchsploit' command available in the Kali Linux distribution.

This command search the ExploitDB database for known exploits targeting various applications and services.

Chapter 5:
Discovery and Exploitation of Vulnerabilities

Exploitation

The "search" command allows direct searching within Metasploit.

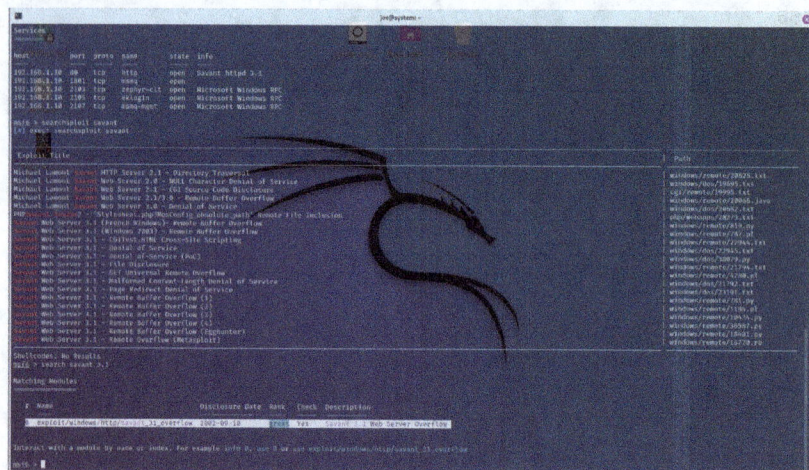

Once you have found a potential exploit, you can use the "info" command followed by the name of the exploit to display detailed information about it. This command will show details about the exploit, including its description, target platform, prerequisites, and the options required to use the exploit.

By examining this information, you will gain a better understanding of how to use the exploit and what options are necessary to customize it for your specific environment.

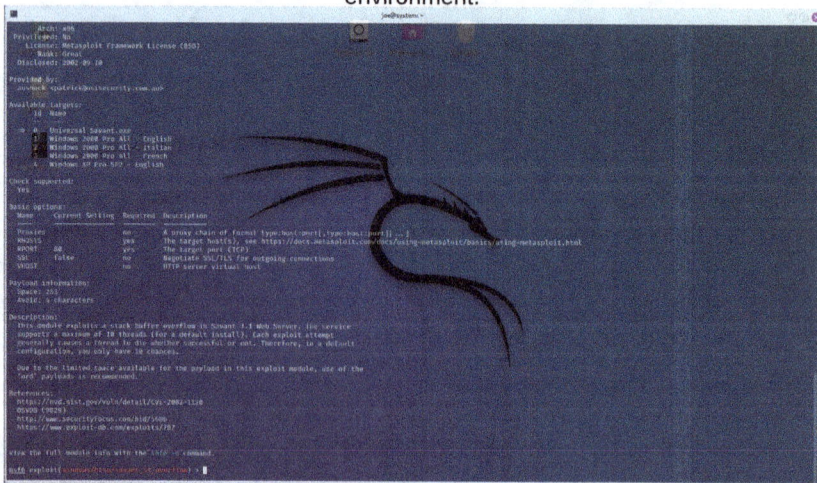

Chapter 5:
Discovery and Exploitation of Vulnerabilities

Exploitation

When using exploits/modules and payloads as part of penetration testing or vulnerability research, it's important to understand the different options that may be required to configure these tools. Indeed, depending on the exploit or payload module used, certain options may be necessary for them to function correctly.

Among the most commonly used options are:

RHOST / RPORT and LHOST / LPORT.

The RHOST option (remote host) is used to specify the IP address of the target you want to attack. If you are conducting a penetration test on a remote machine, you need to specify the IP address of that machine using the RHOST option.

The RPORT option (remote port) is used to specify the port on which the target service is running. You need to know the port number of the target service in order to attack it.

The LHOST option (local host) is used to specify the IP address of your local machine from which you are conducting the attack. This option is used to establish a callback connection with the target machine and to send data from your machine.

The LPORT option (local port) is used to specify the port on which your local machine should listen for callback connections. This option is necessary to establish a callback connection with the target machine and to receive data.

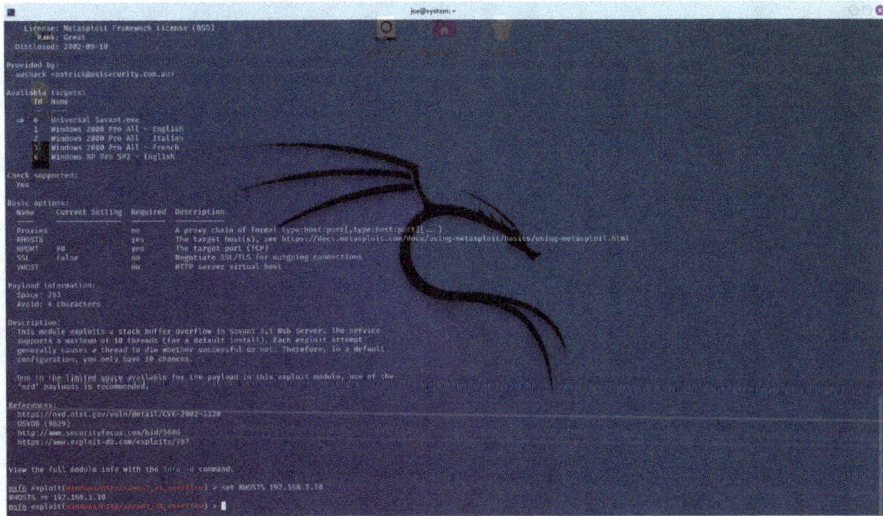

Chapitre 5 :
Discovery and Exploitation of Vulnerabilities

Exploitation

When you use the "show payloads" command in Metasploit, it will display a list of all available payloads for the specific exploit you have selected.

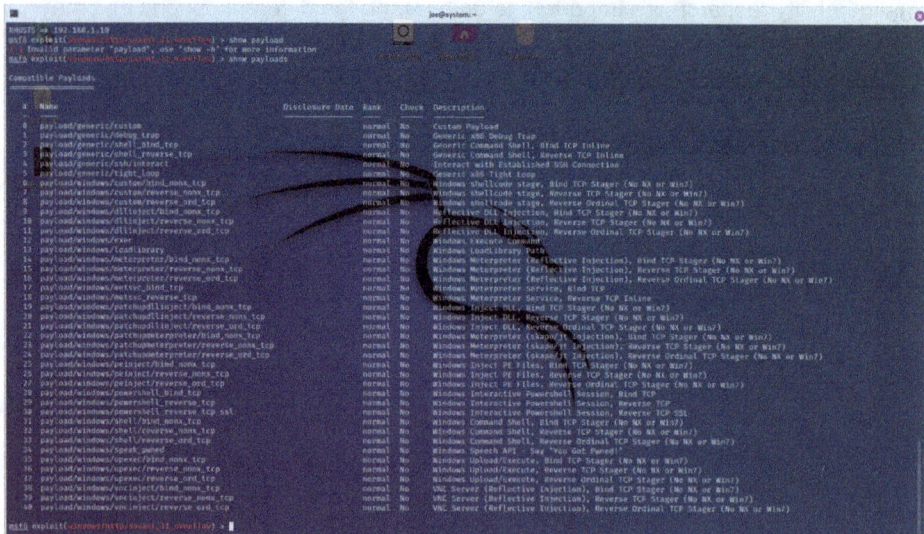

By examining the available payloads for an exploit, you can select the one that best suits your specific environment and the objective of your penetration test. It is important to note that some payloads are more reliable or more discreet than others, and choosing them can impact the success of your exploitation.

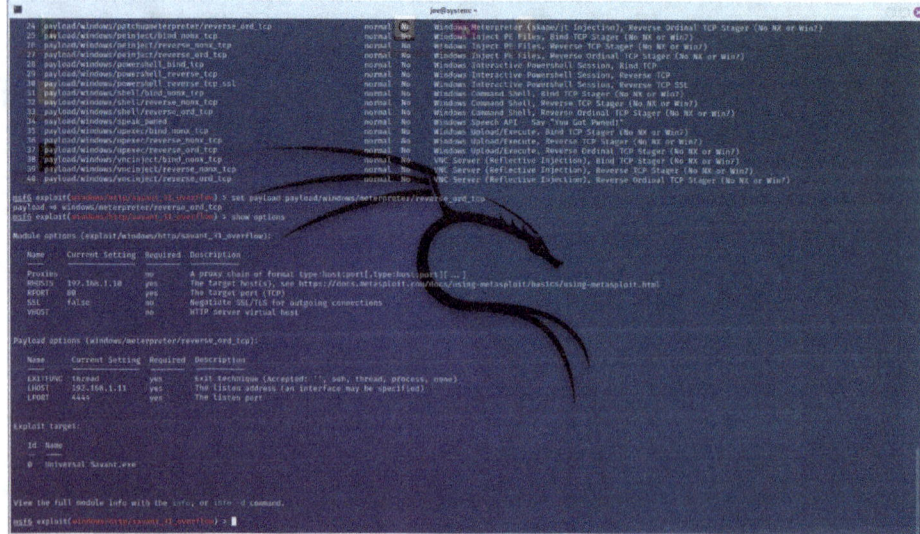

Chapter 5:
Discovery and Exploitation of Vulnerabilities

Exploitation

The "check" command in Metasploit is used to verify if a target is vulnerable to a specific exploit. It allows you to test if the prerequisites for the exploit are met on the target machine, such as software versions, system configurations, open ports, etc.

When a "check" command is available for a specific exploit, it means you can use it to assess the vulnerability of your target before attempting the exploit itself. This saves time and helps avoid potentially dangerous errors when executing an exploit on a non-vulnerable target.

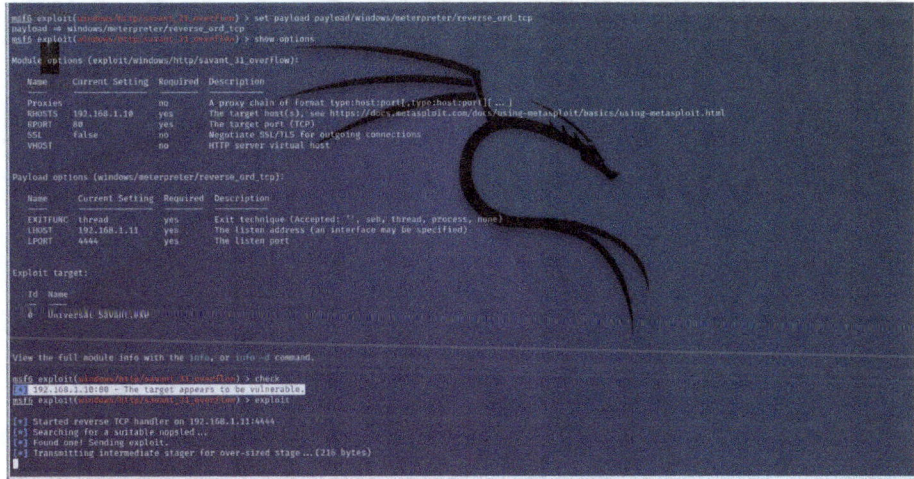

Once you have verified its feasibility using the "check" command, it means that your target is vulnerable and you are ready to launch your attack.

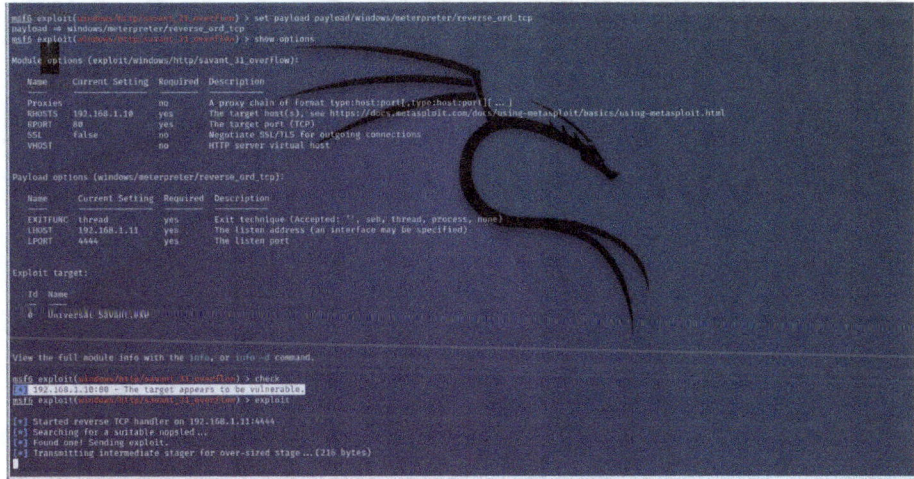

Chapter 5:
Discovery and Exploitation of Vulnerabilities

Exploitation

As you can see in the screenshot, the exploit has been successfully executed and we now have a Meterpreter shell on the target.

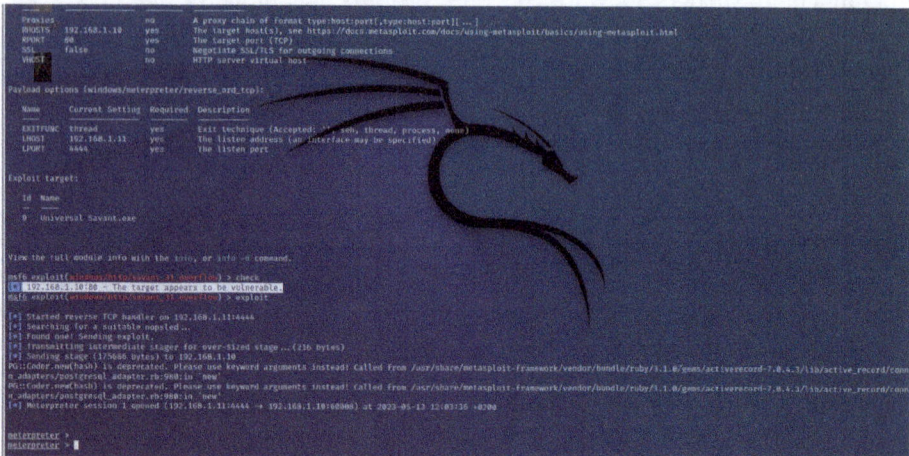

The "shell" command in Meterpreter is a command that provides a system shell on the target machine. This command is very useful because it allows attackers to execute system commands directly on the target machine, as if they were sitting in front of it.

It is important to remember that using a Meterpreter shell for malicious actions is illegal and can lead to legal consequences. Therefore, you should only use this tool to test the security of your own systems or with proper authorization to test the security of other people's systems.

Chapter 5:
Discovery and Exploitation of Vulnerabilities

Post-Exploitation

Once a Meterpreter shell is deployed on a target machine, it offers attackers numerous opportunities to perform malicious actions, including privilege escalation and maintaining access.

Privilege escalation is the process of increasing a user account's privileges to gain higher access levels. This allows attackers to access resources they would not normally have access to. In the context of a Meterpreter shell, this can be achieved by exploiting operating system vulnerabilities or using techniques such as DLL injection, service exploitation, or modifying system files.

There are many tools and techniques that can be used for privilege escalation, including password retrieval tools, operating system vulnerability exploits, and social engineering techniques to obtain credentials.

One popular open-source tool for privilege escalation is Lazagne.py.

It is a password retrieval tool that can recover passwords stored on a target machine, including operating system passwords, web browser passwords, Wi-Fi passwords, and instant messaging passwords.

The "Pivot" module in Metasploit is a feature that allows an attacker to bounce network traffic through a compromised system, also known as "pivoting". This means the attacker can use a compromised system as a starting point to access other systems that are not directly accessible from their original location.

Metasploit's Pivot module uses the Meterpreter shell to create a bidirectional communication channel between the compromised system and the target system, enabling the attacker to control network traffic.

In practice, this means that if an attacker has successfully compromised a system within a company's network, they can use the Pivot module to access other systems within the company that are not directly reachable from the compromised system. This allows the attacker to expand their access and compromise more systems.

Chapter 5:
Discovery and Exploitation of Vulnerabilities

Post-Exploitation

Persistence is a technique that allows an attacker to maintain access to a target machine even after the initial session has been closed.

In the case of Meterpreter, there are several tools to establish persistence on a target machine. One of these tools is "migrate", which allows an attacker to move the Meterpreter process to another running process on the target machine, making it more difficult for the user or system to detect the presence of the attack.

Another commonly used technique for persistence is uploading a backdoor. This involves installing a malicious file on the target machine that can be used to open a remote command session or launch a subsequent attack.

Among other popular tools for installing backdoors on Kali Linux are:

- **Shellter:** a tool that creates backdoors from existing executable files. It also offers obfuscation features to conceal the presence of the backdoor.

- **Veil:** another tool for creating backdoors from existing executable files, with obfuscation features to hide the backdoor.

- **Empire:** a post-exploitation tool for installing persistent backdoors on target machines. It also provides a user-friendly graphical interface for ease of use.

  Covenant: another post-exploitation tool similar to Empire, used for installing persistent backdoors on target machines.

Weevely is a hacking tool that functions differently from other popular backdoor tools on Kali Linux. Specifically, Weevely is a web-based backdoor that allows an attacker to remotely take control of a vulnerable website.(*PHP backdoor*)

Chapter 6
Risk Prevention and
Management

Chapter 6:
Risk Prevention and Management

Now that we have explored various attack and penetration techniquesnt
In this chapter, we will explore different defense solutions and tools to help secure your network and prevent attacks.

- **Education is a key element of cybersecurity** and the best defense against cyberattacks. It is important to raise awareness among users about good security practices, teach them to recognize signs of an attack, and provide them with tools to protect themselves.

- **Every password used should be strong** and unique to avoid brute force/dictionary attacks.

- **To protect your Wi-Fi network:** it is crucial to properly configure your router and follow security best practices. This includes regularly changing the password, disabling non-essential features, and using strong encryption such as WPA2 or preferably WPA3. You can also implement a MAC address filtering policy to only allow approved devices to connect to your Wi-Fi network. Additionally, using tools such as, firewalls, and intrusion detection systems is recommended to monitor your network and detect any suspicious activity.

- **To protect against MITM/MITB attacks**: using VPNs can secure communications and prevent attackers from intercepting network traffic. SSL/TLS certificates can also be used to encrypt communications and ensure the authenticity of the parties involved. Implementing strong authentication protocols, such as Kerberos, can enhance session security and reduce the risk of session hijacking. Use detection tools.

To protect against intrusions on your machine/server:

- Use strong and unique passwords for all your accounts and services, and change them regularly (always).

- Ensure your system is up to date with the latest security updates and vulnerability patches.

- Configure a firewall to block non-essential ports and limit access to services or applications only from authorized IP addresses.

- Use vulnerability scanning tools to identify known vulnerabilities and promptly address them.

- Use intrusion detection tools to monitor suspicious activities on your system or network, and take immediate action if an attack is detected.

- Implement protections against brute force attacks, such as scripts to detect repeated login attempts or tools like fail2ban.

- Use port knocking solutions to obscure access to certain ports on your machine or server to mitigate the risk of attack.

Chapter 6:
Risk Prevention and Management

Protect Your Wi-Fi Network

The security of your Wi-Fi network is crucial to protect your data and privacy. We will review best practices and tools you can use to strengthen the security of your Wi-Fi network.

Firstly, it is essential to properly configure your router.

- **Choose a unique network name (SSID)** and avoid using default network names like "Linksys" or "Netgear". Use a strong and complex password to secure access to your Wi-Fi network, avoiding common words and easily guessed sequences. It is recommended to change the password regularly

- The security of your Wi-Fi network also depends on the encryption used to protect communications between connected devices and the router. **The WPA2 protocol is currently considered the most secure for home Wi-Fi networks and should be used.** If your router supports it, we recommend using WPA3, which is even more secure than WPA2.

- It is also advisable to **disable non-essential features such as WPS (Wi-Fi Protected Setup)**, which can be exploited by attackers to access your network. Additionally, implement a MAC address filtering policy to only allow approved devices to connect to your Wi-Fi network.

In addition to these basic measures,

- **Use tools such as** intrusion detectors, firewalls, and intrusion detection systems to monitor your network and detect any suspicious activity.

- **If your setup allows,** you can limit the range of your Wi-Fi network using directional antennas or by adjusting the signal power to prevent intruders from connecting to your network from outside.

It is recommended to create a separate network for guests or clients to restrict their access to sensitive resources on your main network. You can configure a guest network with limited access permissions and a temporary password for visitors.

The security of your Wi-Fi network depends on several factors such as router configuration, encryption used, disabling non-essential features, implementing MAC address filtering policy, using security tools like intrusion detectors, firewalls, and intrusion detection systems, and limiting the range of your Wi-Fi network. By following these best practices, you can enhance the security

Chapter 6:
Risk Prevention and Management

Protecting Against MITM/MITB Attacks:

Cybersecurity is a critical concern in our increasingly connected world. The risks of cyberattacks are real and can have disastrous consequences, both personally and professionally. Poor security practices can lead to the loss of sensitive data, compromise of systems, invasion of privacy, and even endangerment of personal safety. Therefore, it is essential to implement adequate security measures to protect our information and systems from malicious attacks.

- **Using VPNs** is an effective method to prevent attackers from intercepting network traffic. A VPN creates an encrypted tunnel between your computer and a remote server, acting as a proxy. All network traffic is routed through this tunnel, making it very difficult for an attacker to intercept or manipulate it. VPNs are particularly useful for public Wi-Fi networks or remote connections.

- **SSL/TLS certificates** can also be used to encrypt communications and ensure the authenticity of the parties involved. SSL (Secure Sockets Layer) and TLS (Transport Layer Security) are standard encryption protocols for Internet communications. Websites that use SSL/TLS display a padlock icon in the browser address bar, indicating secure communication. SSL/TLS certificates can be obtained from certification authorities or generated locally.

- **Using strong authentication protocols** such as Kerberos can enhance session security and reduce the risk of session hijacking. Kerberos is a network authentication protocol that uses tickets to validate the identity of users and computers. It is widely used in Microsoft Windows environments but can also be implemented on other platforms.

- **Intrusion detection tools** like Snort can monitor network traffic for suspicious behavior or known attack signatures. Snort is an open-source intrusion detection system that can be configured to alert administrators to suspicious activity or attempted attacks. Other intrusion detection tools include Bro, Suricata, and OSSEC.

It is important to note that these measures are not exhaustive, and security should be considered an ongoing process. Attackers can always find ways to circumvent security measures, so it is crucial to remain vigilant and regularly update security tools.

Chapter 6:
Risk Prevention and Management

Protecting Against Intrusions on Your Machine / Server

To protect your machine/server against potential attacks, it is recommended to implement a strict security policy:

- It is important to keep your **system and antivirus (AV) up to date** by regularly installing security updates and vulnerability patches.

- You can implement tools to **detect scanning attempts or brute force attacks, such as Fail2ban or custom brute force detection scripts.**

- Additionally, consider **disabling unnecessary services, such as unused open ports,**

- **Configure firewall rules** properly to restrict access to necessary services.

- **Using strong authentication systems**, such as two-factor authentication (2FA), can also enhance the security of your machine or server.

As always, it is crucial to enforce a strong password security policy by using complex and unique passwords for each service or account.

Port Knocking:

Port knocking is a security technique that hides the opening of ports using a secret sequence of connections.

The principle involves closing ports on your machine or server, for example, port 22 (ssh). When a user wants to open a specific port, they must send a sequence of connections to specific ports in a precise order. This sequence is pre-configured and known only to the authorized user.

When the sequence of connections is detected, the firewall or security system automatically opens the specified port for the user. This makes accessing ports on your machine or server more challenging for attackers since they do not know the connection sequence.

Port knocking can be configured for a sequence of connections involving two, three, four, or more ports. It is a simple and effective method to add an additional layer of security to your machine or server.

However, it is important to note that the security of port knocking depends on the complexity of the sequence and the authorized user's ability to remember it.

Chapter 6:
Risk Prevention and Management

It is true that hackers like to exploit software for their advantage. You can do the same!

By performing a simple port scan in the correct order, it is possible to execute a script or program instead of just opening a port.

This can offer them a wide range of defensive possibilities, such as:

- Temporarily opening a port to allow remote users to connect to a specific service.

- Initiating automatic data backup to a remote server.

- Modifying router configuration remotely without the need to open a permanent port.

- Triggering a security action, script, or other process.

- Using port knocking to open a backdoor and remotely access the target machine.

- Executing scripts remotely without the need to establish a direct connection.

- Closing a specific port or service once the connection has been established to limit intrusion risks.

- Monitoring port and service usage to detect any suspicious activity.

- Restricting access to ports and services only to authorized IP addresses.

I would like to express my sincere thanks to you, dear reader, for reading this book on hacking.

I hope you have found the information and tools presented in this book helpful and relevant to your projects and learning.

Hacking is a complex and ever-evolving subject, and it is important to be well-informed and prepared to navigate this field.

I hope this book has contributed to giving you a better understanding of hacking concepts and techniques, as well as the security measures to protect your own systems and networks.

If you have any questions or feedback regarding the content of this book, I encourage you to contact me via Twitter or Instagram. I am always happy to engage with people interested in hacking and to share knowledge and experiences.

I would also like to thank everyone who contributed to the creation of this book, including databook, my friends (especially Sylvain alias Kor-dev and Nelson from Xartists ;), my family, and my wife Sam who supported me throughout this project.

In conclusion, I hope this book has been valuable to you and that you enjoyed reading it. Thank you again for taking the time to read it, and I wish you all the best in your future security endeavors.

Best regards,

Julien B.

Twitter : JulienBones @Datab0ok

www.ingramcontent.com/pod-product-compliance
Lightning Source LLC
Chambersburg PA
CBHW071938210526
45479CB00002B/733